Cambridge Elements ≡

Elements in the Economics of Emerging Markets
edited by
Bruno S. Sergi
Harvard University

EXCHANGE RATES IN SOUTH AMERICA'S EMERGING MARKETS

Luis Molinas Sosa
Central Bank of Paraguay

Caio Vigo Pereira
University of Kansas

CAMBRIDGE
UNIVERSITY PRESS

CAMBRIDGE
UNIVERSITY PRESS

University Printing House, Cambridge CB2 8BS, United Kingdom

One Liberty Plaza, 20th Floor, New York, NY 10006, USA

477 Williamstown Road, Port Melbourne, VIC 3207, Australia

314–321, 3rd Floor, Plot 3, Splendor Forum, Jasola District Centre, New Delhi – 110025, India

79 Anson Road, #06–04/06, Singapore 079906

Cambridge University Press is part of the University of Cambridge.

It furthers the University's mission by disseminating knowledge in the pursuit of education, learning, and research at the highest international levels of excellence.

www.cambridge.org
Information on this title: www.cambridge.org/9781108810135
DOI: 10.1017/9781108893671

First published 2020

A catalogue record for this publication is available from the British Library.

ISBN 978-1-108-81013-5 Paperback
ISSN 2631-8598 (online)
ISSN 2631-858X (print)

Cambridge University Press has no responsibility for the persistence or accuracy of URLs for external or third-party internet websites referred to in this publication and does not guarantee that any content on such websites is, or will remain, accurate or appropriate.

Exchange Rates in South America's Emerging Markets

Elements in the Economics of Emerging Markets

DOI: 10.1017/9781108893671
First published online: June 2020

Luis Molinas Sosa
Central Bank of Paraguay

Caio Vigo Pereira
University of Kansas

Author for correspondence: Luis Molinas Sosa, lmolinas@bcp.gov.py

Abstract: Since Meese and Rogoff's (1983) work, results have shown that no model could outperform a random walk in predicting exchange rates. Many papers have tried to find a forecasting methodology that could beat the random walk, at least for certain forecasting periods. This Element compares the Purchasing Power Parity, the Uncovered Interest Rate, the Sticky Price, the Bayesian Model Averaging, and the Bayesian Vector Autoregression models to the random walk benchmark in forecasting exchange rates between most South American currencies and the US dollar, and between the Paraguayan guarani and the Brazilian real and the Argentinian peso. Forecasts are evaluated under the criteria of Root Mean Square Error, Direction of Change, and the Diebold-Mariano statistic. The results indicate that the two Bayesian models have greater forecasting power and that there is little evidence in favor of using the other three fundamentals models, except purchasing power parity at longer forecasting horizons.

Keywords: Forecasting, Exchange rates, Bayesian model averaging, Bayesian vector autoregression, Purchasing power parity, Uncovered interest rate, Sticky price

ISBNs: 9781108810135 (PB), 9781108893671 (OC)
ISSNs: 2631-8598 (online), ISSN 2631-858X (print)

Contents

1 Introduction

Exchange rate forecasting is a complicated matter. It has been the subject of many studies that have yielded promising results only to be subsequently refuted by others. Attempts at formal exchange rate forecasting have existed for more than a century. For instance, purchasing power parity (PPP) was developed into a theory of exchange rate behavior by the early twentieth century in Cassel (1918a). By the 1960s, as discussed in the next section, it was already the subject of "appraisals." In the same vein, the uncovered interest rate parity (UIP) model has been part of the discussion since Keynes (1923). Both of these models are still workhorses in international finance courses all over the world. The 1970s saw a burst of activity in exchange rate forecasting theory, with several models developed one after the other – an activity that spilled into the early 1980s. And yet, a definitive model or framework remains elusive. In particular, since Meese and Rogoff (1983) argued that no model outperforms a driftless random walk in forecasting exchange rates (a phenomenon known from then on as the "Meese and Rogoff puzzle"), researchers have been forced to go back to the drawing board to come up with more solid alternatives. The idea of efficient markets and the impossibility of predicting asset prices consistently dates back to Malkiel and Fama (1970), but it took a few years before it made its way into international finance. It should be noted, however, that Meese and Rogoff's work does not exactly lend direct support to the efficient market hypothesis (EMH). EMH says the exchange rate today is the best guess for tomorrow's exchange rate, but it also implies that exchange rates are not related to economic fundamentals. Meese and Rogoff do not imply the latter part. It is in light of all this that, for the following three decades, economists would go back and forth in arguing for and against the possibility of forecasting exchange rates. For instance, Lothian and Wu (2011) show that the UIP has remarkable forecasting power in longer time horizons. But studies such as Cheung et al. (2005) have reinforced the idea that no model can consistently beat a random walk, as they find that even when models produce improved forecasts, these improvements are not statistically significant. At the same time, they find that no model (or predictor) works consistently better for all the countries they consider. This fact makes the study of emerging markets (those of South America, in this case) all the more important.

The objective of this Element is to evaluate the predictability of these standard models in addition to two Bayesian approaches to the South American case. We make a modest contribution to the literature by expanding on the results obtained by Wright (2008) and extending the framework of Lam et al. (2008) to produce a regional application. Both studies used Bayesian

Model Averaging (BMA) to forecast the exchange rates of the US dollar (USD) with respect to several other currencies and then compare them to the performance of a benchmark model, namely, the driftless random walk. In particular, Lam et al. (2008) added three other structural models besides BMA and compared them to the random walk as well. These models are the aforementioned PPP model, the UIP model, and the sticky price (SP) model. They are well-known models in the literature and have been extensively discussed, both in the past and in recent years (see next section). It is this latter approach that we have followed for this Element, in conjunction with a Bayesian Vector Autoregression (BVAR) model with a Minnesota prior. As Carriero et al. (2009) show, BVAR models perform well in the long and the short runs, including one period ahead forecasts. To assess the performance of each model, we evaluate the root mean square error (RMSE) ratio generated by each model and the direction of change (DoC) ratio, and we also perform the Diebold-Mariano (DM) test for statistical significance.

More specifically, we have used the previously mentioned models to forecast the exchange rates between the Argentinian peso (ARS), the Brazilian real (BRL), the Bolivian boliviano (BOB), the Chilean peso (CLP), the Colombian peso (COP), and the Paraguayan guarani (PYG) against the USD. We also produce forecasts for the PYG against the BRL and ARS, as these are the founding members of the economic bloc known as the Common Market of the South (MERCOSUR). It also adds some variety to the experiment. We use monthly data. Unlike Wright (2008), we do not separate the variables into a financial and a macroeconomic data set to estimate monthly and quarterly exchange rates, respectively – all variables are monthly. Lam et al. (2008) only produced forecasts based on quarterly data. The forecasting periods are 3, 6, 9, and 12 months ahead. Some results are encouraging and in line with Wright's work but appear to be at odds with Lothian and Wu's study as UIP does perform especially well in the longer run. Results do agree with Carriero et al. (2009) under the RMSE criterion. More specifically, in all cases except that of the BOB/USD, CLP/USD, and PYG/ARS, BMA outperforms all other models in the 3-month horizon; in all cases and for all forecasting horizons, BVAR outperforms the random walk (except BOB/USD and PYG/USD for the 6-month and 9-month horizons); in about half the cases, PPP, UIP, and SP outperform all other models in the 12-month horizon. In the 6- and 9-month horizons, the performance of almost all models is mixed (except BVAR). Results are somewhat similar under the DoC criterion, but some of the fundamentals models do have a better performance when predicting the direction of change. In the case of Argentina, for instance, UIP, PPP, and SP appear to fare far better under both criteria, owing perhaps to Argentina's recent and complex history of inflation and price and exchange rate volatility. On the other hand, BOB/USD shows decidedly mixed results, with the consistently worst performance under RMSE but a much better one under DoC. Under the DM criterion, some forecasts are statistically significant improvements in the 3-month horizon in the cases of BMA and BVAR, and only in the case of BVAR for all horizons (but not for all exchange rates). The structural models produce improved forecasts that are statistically significant only in a few forecasting periods and only for a handful of currencies, where SP is the worst-performing model. UIP only produces some statistically significant improvements if we extend the forecasting horizon to two years.

More generally, this Element could be of interest to academicians who work on exchange rate forecasting – in particular, if they focus on emerging markets. Policy makers in central banks, statistics institutes, and other governmental institutions (especially those in South America but certainly in any country that is a big importer or exporter of commodities) might also find some use for the results presented here.

The rest of the Element proceeds as follows: in Section 2, we discuss the monetary history of the countries under consideration; in Section 3, we discuss the previous literature related to exchange rate forecasting; in Section 4, we describe the models and the motivation for their choice; in Section 5, we describe the data and their sources; in Section 6, we present the results, briefly discuss them, and suggest possible further research. Finally, in Section 7, we conclude.

2 Historical Background

This section offers a short summary of the monetary history of the countries whose exchange rates we are considering. These summaries will give context to the present study and the circumstances in which exchange rates show their respective behaviors.

2.1 Argentina

As the Central Bank of the Argentine Republic (BCRA) reports until 1881, the country's monetary and financial system was characterized by the coexistence of a multiplicity of currencies issued by different banks in the country or abroad.[1] In that year, a national currency was established and linked to the gold standard, but the convertibility was ephemeral, and the "quasi-currencies" continued to circulate.

---

[1] See www.bcra.gob.ar/Institucional/Historia.asp. We refer to this document as (BCRA, n.d.) where n.d. means "not dated."

At the beginning of the twentieth century, after several crises associated with external indebtedness, the country was able to return to the gold standard and established a rigid link between the balance of payments and the amount of money in circulation (BCRA, n.d.). The outbreak of the banking crisis of 1890–1 motivated the creation of institutions such as the Conversion Office and the National Bank, which, until the 1930s, centralized instruments and functions that would later be given over to the Central Bank.

At the beginning of the international financial crisis of 1929, the country's monetary and financial system did not do well. The crisis forced the establishment of exchange controls and other measures of state intervention in an abandonment of free trade postulates. In that context, and due to its repercussions on the banking system, the conditions were created for the founding of a central bank that would be responsible for centralizing the control of monetary and exchange rate policy (BCRA, n.d.).

In 1959, the government launched a plan that aimed at reducing the inflation rate. During the first half of the 1960–76 period, Argentina heavily regulated the domestic financial markets and was closed to international capital movements, according to Buera and Nicolini (2019).

Starting in 1970, the healthy downward trend in the deficit reverted, and it started growing every year, reaching a record high of 11 percent of GDP by 1975. The government established policies of price controls and generated shortages of products that characterized those years. In 1975, the government eliminated price controls, and inflation started to rise again; during several months in 1975 and 1976, it reached values between 300 percent and 700 percent annually, as explained in Buera and Nicolini (2019). According to the authors, the government did not have access to international credit markets in this period, so the fiscal deficit was the main driver of the inflation rate. As the fiscal deficit spun out of control by 1975, so did the inflation rate.

In the 1977–80 period, the government started a deregulation policy, reducing trade barriers, deregulating the domestic credit market, and liberalizing capital accounts. These decisions allowed the government to finance its deficit abroad. These changes prompted many banks to enter the market, and the financial sector's size increased as a proportion of GDP (see Buera and Nicolini (2019)).

To stop inflation gradually, the government decided to adopt a crawling-peg system, which announced decreasing devaluation rates of the peso against the US dollar. With the crawling-peg system, the inflation rate decreased more than 700 percent in 1976. Inflation declined until 1981, in spite of increasing deficits. Those deficits and contingent liabilities led to higher debt, high inflation, and a government default in 1982. This situation forced the government to be out of the international capital markets until the 1990s, and seigniorage financed the fiscal imbalances, according to Buera and Nicolini (2019).

In the 1975–82 period, the exchange rate devalued more than 200,000 percent, and the government had to print 1 million Peso Ley 18.188 bills (CACS, 2018). Singh (2005) mentions that none of the larger countries in Latin America had an annual inflation rate less than 20 percent during 1980s. In fact, Argentina, Bolivia, and Brazil experienced periods of hyperinflation. Argentina had an extreme experience in the region with an average inflation rate of 350 percent during the decade, consumer prices increasing by a factor of more than 100 million.

In 1983, due to the high inflation levels registered in 1975–82, the government decided to replace the Peso Ley with a new currency. Therefore, the peso argentino appeared and was equivalent to 10,000 Pesos Ley 18.188 (CACS, 2018). However, inflation reached an average of 650 percent annually, and the peso argentino lost its value. In 1985, the government decided to change the national currency again and the Austral appeared. With this regime, one Austral was equivalent to 1,000 pesos argentinos (CACS, 2018).

The Austral Plan brought down inflation, and a fiscal effort drove the deficit down to 3.7 percent and 2.9 percent of GDP in 1985 and 1986, respectively. This effort was short lived though, and the deficit grew to around 5 percent in the following three years. Consequently, a new hyperinflation period began in 1989. Almost 90 percent of the lending capacity of the banking sector went toward financing the government (see Buera and Nicolini (2019)).

In 1989, the Austral had devalued 4,700 percent with respect to the US dollar; in 1991, the peso (a new one) was issued. In March, the government established the exchange rate parity against the US dollar, and one peso was equivalent to 10,000 Australes. The exchange rate parity with the US dollar lasted until 2002 (CACS, 2018).

The beginning of 1990 was dramatic. In March, inflation reached 100 percent monthly. By the end of the year, the overall rate exceeded 700 percent, according to Buera and Nicolini (2019). Starting in 1991, Argentina reduced its inflation from more than 700 percent to less than 10 percent by mid-1993 (see Singh (2005)). The government signed the Brady Plan in 1993. This plan's objective was to restructure the defaulted debt and transform it into sovereign bonds. Following the plan, the government was able to borrow in international markets, per Buera and Nicolini (2019).

In 1995, a bank run began; in five months, the deposits in the banking sector fell by 20 percent. This crisis was further complicated by the limited action taken by the central bank. In 1998, Argentina experienced a reversal of fortunes in its current account following an international crisis. In that year, the recession ended a strong recovery (GDP had been growing 6 percent annually). By 2002, GDP had declined 18 percent, unemployment reached unprecedented levels, and poverty rates rose above 40 percent. The recovery from this great recession was fast and accompanied by six years of fiscal surpluses (see Buera and Nicolini (2019)). Finally, in the 2008–10 period, the healthy surpluses disappeared and turned into deficits that reached 6 percent by 2017. However, an agreement with bondholders allowed the government to continue to borrow abroad.

2.2 Brazil

In what follows, we will go through the many stabilization and development plans and processes that Brazil experienced from 1960 to 2016. At the beginning of the1960s, the Bank of Brazil was the monetary authority in the country and played a role as a commercial bank, lending credits to the manufacturing and agricultural sectors and intervening in the foreign exchange market. The main source to cover the considerable fiscal deficit was the seignorage revenue. At that time, Brazil suffered from a deeply complicated inflationary crisis because of the expansion of the monetary base, according to Ayres et al. (2019).

The same work describes the monetary plans implemented by the government. First, the Targets Plan, announced during the presidency of Juscelino Kubitshchek (1956–61), had the objective of providing an adequate infrastructure to industrialize Brazil. In the first years, the country experienced high growth rates in real GDP, but the plan failed because of high inflation and the growing fiscal deficit. To deal with high inflation and low growth, the government launched a second Plan of Government Economic Action (PAEG) in 1964. Through fiscal and financial reforms, the Central Bank of Brazil (BCB) was created with the purpose of separating the commercial role that the Bank of Brazil had at that time. This allowed Brazil to reduce its fiscal deficits by increasing the tax revenue to almost 23 percent of GDP. However, the separation was not complete, because the government settled a dispute between the Bank of Brazil and the Central Bank, giving the Bank of Brazil the power to issue money.

After the PAEG implementation, the government reduced its revenues from seigniorage, stabilized inflation, and reduced money growth. The years from 1964 to 1973 were known as the "economic miracle," with growth rates of about 10 percent annually and a number of infrastructure projects underway. In 1973, after the first oil crisis, inflation, seigniorage revenues, and monetary growth started to rise, and the government debt was increased to maintain growth during this crisis.

In the first half of the 1980s, the objective was to reduce external imbalances, notwithstanding the rising inflation that reached more than 100 percent. Policies implemented by President João Figueiredo increased the government debt securities indexed to inflation and reduced the stock of public domestic debt. The nominal interest rate was low, because of the growth of the monetary base. The Cruzado Plan was a stabilization plan, implemented in February 1986. The idea was to change the currency denomination from cruzeiro to cruzado by eliminating three zeros, freezing prices to keep a "zero inflation objective," and allowing indexation only for periods of more than one year. To prevent a recession risk, salaries were adjusted to their real average value of the previous six months. In the case of the exchange rate, the currency was attached to the US dollar, as mentioned in Ladefroux (1994). The author explains some of the consequences of the Cruzado Plan. At first, salary revenues were higher, causing an accelerated demand that overheated the market. Then, basic products began to become scarce, and the black market was the only source that could satisfy the demand, especially from the wealthy social strata.

Eventually, all stores ran out of products and a corrective plan named Cruzado II was launched after the presidential election. A tax increase on cars, cigarettes, alcoholic drinks, and public services was decreed, which was unpopular all over the country. This rise in prices was accompanied by social upheaval.

In July 1987, the government announced a new plan called the Brasser Plan. It decreed a new freeze in prices, and the economic team established a salary indexation called "price reference unit," which was adjusted for the following three months according to the inflation average, causing a gap between the adjustment and inflation, as Ayres et al. (2019) explain. Ladefroux (1994) mentions why the plan was not successful: inflation rates reached 366 percent at the end of 1987; an average worker from São Paulo (Brazil's largest city) had to work 204 hours to buy a basic basket of goods.

At the beginning of 1988, a new minister implemented a new economic policy called *Feijão com Arroz* (Rice with Beans), with the objective of keeping inflation at 15 percent per month. This policy succeeded at first, but then inflation increased again, surpassing the 15 percent objective.

In January 1989, the government tried again to establish a successful plan, freezing prices one more time and establishing a fixed exchange rate for an indefinite time and a de-indexation plan. However, the government had no support from Congress, and the plan was dismissed. Meanwhile, at the end of the 1980s, inflation rates were at 70 percent per month according to Ayres et al. (2019). Moreover, in 1989, the government substituted its currency again, dropping the cruzado for the "novo cruzado."

In 1990, Fernando Collor de Melo was elected president and announced the Collor Plan, which had been considered the most ambitious plan ever adopted to rebuild the national economy. The plan aimed at deficit reduction, without an extreme cut in public investment, to end hyperinflation. It increased the tax on financial intermediation, suspended tax incentives, and froze prices. The plan was conceived to roll out in two stages: the first would reduce the money supply and the second would reduce the fiscal deficit, as explained by Marongiu (2007). This new reform substituted the novo cruzado with cruzeiros, blocking the novo cruzado monetary base. Meanwhile, 70 percent of this base could only be used to pay previous debts. The remaining 30 percent was converted to cruzeiros, after applying an 8 percent tax rate. The controversial side of the plan, according to Ladefroux (1994), was that savings accounts with 50,000 cruzeiros or more were retained for eighteen months to be invested in federal government bonds. As Pereira and Nakano (1991) explain, the plan produced a mild recession, related to the reduction of the money supply. First, production fell in April and then started to increase but fell again in August. Plan Collor did not adopt measures to stop inflation – on the contrary, it contributed to triggering a rise in it. A second stage, Plan Collor II, froze prices and salaries again and increased tariffs on public services to balance public accounts. There was a reduction in the rate of inflation growth; however, when financial assets were released, inflation started growing again, as Marongiu (2007) explains.

Ayres et al. (2019) tell us that in 1994, the last and most ambitious plan of stabilization was launched: the Real Plan. It did not freeze prices, unlike previous plans. It began with the congressional approval of an Emergency Social Fund, which allowed the government to increase by 20 percent the revenues at its disposal – before that, those funds were designated to different areas. Then, the real value unity (URV) was adopted as a new unit of account in parity with the dollar, establishing a daily conversion rate of URVs to cruzeiros. The plan was very successful, as it affected inflationary expectations and indexed salaries to inflation, which allowed the next step to be followed: the implementation of the real as the new currency in July 1994 (see Baumann and Fialho Mussi (1999)).

The results after the full implementation were notorious. The inflation rate decreased from 40 percent per month in 1993 to 2 percent in 1998. This disinflation led the country to experience GDP growth rates of 4 percent during the first semester in 1994 and 6 percent in the second semester. These rates could not be sustained because of external shocks such as the Mexican crisis in 1995, the Asian crisis in 1997, the Russian crisis in 1998, and a speculative attack on the real that made the Central Bank change the crawling-peg regime to a floating exchange rate regime. This change was accompanied by the implementation of the inflation-targeting regime that is still used today as the main monetary policy tool, according to Baumann and Fialho Mussi (1999).

Finally, in this century, the boom in commodity prices led Brazil to experience high growth rates of real GDP per capita that eventually fell when this boom ended. Meanwhile, multiple social programs and increased investments and interventions in state-owned enterprises caused a fiscal deterioration, as explained by Ayres et al. (2019).

2.3 Bolivia

The Central Bank of Bolivia (n.d.) relates how in the 1913–17 period, during Ismael Montes's presidency, the Bolivian National Bank centralized the boliviano (the Bolivian currency) emission until 1928, when the Central Bank of Bolivia was created. In 1945, with its charter emission, the Central Bank of Bolivia was charged with controlling inflation and promoting national growth.

Until 1956, Bolivia's monetary and fiscal policies were expansive, and the objective, according to Sheriff and Ernesto (1992), was to compensate for the small domestic market and reduce social pressures. The authors state that an inflationary period began as a result of an expansion in payments methods, and GDP fell because of poor agricultural production. In December 1956, the government initiated a monetary stabilization program. The Eder Plan (as it was known) was successful and slowed inflation until 1972. In this sixteen-year period, inflation was even negative in some years. Kehoe et al. (2019) comment that the government looked to reduce the liquidity available in the economy by cutting public expenditures and loans and liberalizing prices.

Molina argues that the Eder Plan was not applied as originally designed, because his methods would lead to a recession. Whatever the case, monetary supply was controlled, inflation was reduced 100 percent, and the exchange rate was stabilized at 12,000 bolivianos per US dollar.

In the 1960–9 period, the Bolivian economy grew by 3 percent in terms of GDP per capita; the Eder Plan made this possible by controlling inflation. Inflation was reduced from 178 percent in 1956 to 11.5 percent in 1960, as explained in Kehoe et al. (2019).

As a result of inflation, Víctor Paz Estenssoro's government had to reform the monetary system, and in 1962 the peso boliviano appeared (Central Bank of Bolivia (n.d.)). The fixed exchange rate also influenced the determination to replace bolivianos; the peso boliviano was equivalent to 1,000 bolivianos. In the following years, the country experienced an impressive expansion period, according to Mortimore (1981). Bolivia, in the mid-1970s, presented the common characteristics of a crisis. In 1975, exports decreased by 3.4 percent and the external debt increased by 23.8 percent. By 1976, net domestic investment had decreased by 6.7 percent.

At the beginning of 1970, Bolivia received large inflows of credit from international banks loans. However, in the 1980s, external credit was constrained, interest rates were high, and a global recession and internal political chaos ensued (see Kehoe et al. (2019)). To overcome the debt crisis, the government had to finance its expenditures through the Central Bank (Central Bank of Bolivia (n.d.)). Between 1983 and 1984, the Central Bank's credit represented 18 percent of the GDP.

At the start of the 1980s, Bolivia suffered its worst inflationary period, which was one of the most remarkable worldwide. The Central Bank had to print 100,000 peso boliviano bills and management checks (checks guaranteed with the Central Bank's own funds) equivalent to 1 million pesos bolivianos (Central Bank of Bolivia (n.d.)). Humérez Quiroz and Ayaviri (2005) explain that during this decade, economic activity grew on average 0.1 percent as a consequence of the 1982 and 1986 recessions. According to Kehoe et al. (2019), an economic, political, and social crisis began in the aftermath of the end of the military regime (1964–82).

Disinvestment, financial obligations, and external debt brought about Bolivia's most severe crisis. The 1985 crisis brought unemployment, hyperinflation, and terrible living conditions. In 1985, the country faced its most significant price increases (Central Bank of Bolivia (n.d.)).

Sachs (1987) mentions that Bolivia's inflation rate in 1984–5 was one of the highest in the world and the fastest growing in the region's history. In just one year, inflation rose 20,000 percent; in the last four months of the hyperinflationary period, it reached 60,000 percent annually. The author also mentions that the Bolivian inflation was a case of true hyperinflation, as, according to Cagan (1956), hyperinflation consists of inflation rates higher than 50 percent monthly. In November 1986, the 901 Law changed the monetary regime. Bolivianos replaced pesos bolivianos and the economy gradually stabilized.

Fast forward to 1999, when a slowdown of the economy created social and political conflicts. Three years later, in 2002, after a presidential election, the country experienced a huge outflow of deposits as a result of an unexpected outcome in presidential elections, and the financial system lost 23 percent of total deposits, as reported by Kehoe et al. (2019).

In 2002 and 2003, the deficit reached 9 percent and 8 percent of GDP, respectively. Pension expenses and fuel subsidies represented 75 percent of the deficit and were financed through external debt. International agencies granted credits with the objective of controlling the fiscal deficit (Central Bank of Bolivia (n.d.)).

Kehoe et al. (2019) explain that as the fiscal deficit reached unsustainable levels, the government implemented an income tax, generating popular rejection. In October, as a consequence of social crises and after losing its legitimacy, the new government resigned. Eventually, Bolivia experienced an exports boom in 2003. Prices of Bolivian exports increased as well as natural gas exports to Brazil. Bolivia recovered from the recession when the international crisis ended and the natural gas industry rebounded.

In 2005, Evo Morales was elected president; one year later, his government began the process of nationalizing oil, electricity, and telecommunications companies. The high commodity prices allowed Bolivia to experience a nonfinancial public sector surplus in the 2006–13 period, as per Kehoe et al. (2019). According to the authors, this year was important for Bolivia, since, during a meeting of the G8 countries, complete debt forgiveness for the country was announced. The Bolivian Central Bank was able to accumulate reserves. Net international reserves increased from 12.0 percent of GDP in 2003 to 51.8 percent of GDP in 2012. Finally, by 2007, international reserves represented 27.5 percent of GDP and the fiscal deficit reached 7.8 percent of GDP.

Bolivia's fiscal income went through an important expansion in the 2006–13 period, which caused a strong growth in domestic demand (Central Bank of Bolivia (n.d.)). This situation partially explains its production growth. According to Kehoe et al. (2019), the fiscal deficit is currently growing and international reserves are falling; these are troubling similarities to the 1970s.

2.4 Chile

It is important to include a brief review of the background of the Central Bank of Chile and its creation as one of the first in Latin America and afterward the evolution of the monetary history of Chile. The Central Bank of Chile was created in 1925 as an institution that could provide business liquidity to the banks and foreign exchange rate stability and maintain confidence in monetary policy (see Canto 1942). The first central bank regime was the gold standard, abandoned in 1931 during the Great Depression, and followed by the establishment of multiples exchanges, exchange controls, and protectionism. The years following the Great Depression were accompanied by macro stability and low inflation rates, according to Corbo and Hernández (2005). The authors of this work explain that during the period 1932–52, however, there was a credit expansion, as a result of the financing by the central bank of public and private institutions. This caused high inflation rates that reached 80 percent during 1953–5, and the fiscal deficit increased. During this period, the main tools for managing inflation were price controls, fixed exchange rates, and readjustment of salaries.

In 1955, Chile took a hard look at the inflation problem and detected the main causes: the fiscal deficit, monetary expansion, the exchange rate policy, and the wage rate policy. In 1958, during the presidency of Jorge Alessandri, a stabilization plan was released, which aimed to reverse the fiscal deficit, fix the exchange rate to the dollar, and adjust wages, reducing inflation. Nevertheless, the fiscal deficit and inflation started to rise again, the fixed exchange rate was abandoned, and the nominal exchange rate suffered a deep depreciation, according to Caputo and Saravia (2018). As per the same work, Eduardo Frei, elected president in 1964, presented many plans that included investment in infrastructure and social areas and an increase in real wages. A gradual stabilization plan, expected to reduce inflation to 10 percent by the third year, was also part of the plan. The plan failed three years later, with an inflation average of 25 percent due to the scarce level of national investment and the high wage adjustment.

In 1970, many socialist parties joined to the "Unidad Popular" (Popular Unity) organization and presented Salvador Allende as their candidate. He was elected president in that year. When he assumed the presidency, he promoted an economic plan that included the nationalization of banks and industries and the expansion of the government. An aggressive expansion in 1971 increased aggregate demand. This led to a real GDP growth of 9.4 percent; meanwhile, inflation was contained due to price controls. GDP growth did not continue and fell in 1972. The fiscal deficit reached 23 percent and hyperinflation reached 433 percent in 1973. In addition, foreign reserves fell to finance the expansion of government expenditure (see Caputo and Saravia (2018)).

In September 1973, a military coup in Chile installed a military dictatorship led by Augusto Pinochet that lasted until 1990. Pinochet's regime would implement controversial economic reforms (see, for instance, Lebdioui (2019)). The government had as economic counselors (the military occupied high positions) a group of economists who had studied in Chicago in the 1960s. They had the idea of applying free market postulates in Chile and worked on reforms that could cover all economic areas, according to Fontaine (1993). This work enumerates what those reforms included: changing the government's size; reducing the fiscal deficit and taxes; eliminating price controls; initiating the privatization of the state-owned enterprises, including social security, education, and health; creating a low and uniform tax structure to open the economy to the world through the reduction of exchange controls and the elimination of imports; liberalizing foreign investment; creating an independent central bank; encouraging a flexible labor market through the reduction of the power of workers unions, the reduction of entrance barriers, layoffs, and government intervention in the labor market; and creating efficient social programs to attack poverty.

French-Davis (2003) mentions positive and negative aspects of the reforms. The results during the dictatorship were lower than expected: GDP grew 2.9 percent on average and GDP per capita fell 3 percent. The salary gap between the lower class and the highest earners increased, and the unemployment rate reached its highest level since the 1960s. The 1980s saw worsening economic conditions and mounting international pressure for Pinochet's regime to become more democratic, including pressure from the Catholic Church. Pinochet called a referendum in 1988 that asked for a ten-year extension of his regime. He lost the referendum and was voted out of power the following year. According to the same work, the economy showed great results in the democratic period that began in 1990. GDP grew 7.1 percent on average during the first eight years and brought a reduction in the poverty rate and a rise of the minimum salary. New reforms were also introduced in the labor market that protected workers and increased taxes. To prevent the economy from returning to the great recessions of the dictatorship, the government worked to maintain a stable aggregate demand, synchronized with production capability, coupled with balanced foreign accounts and a reduction of the fiscal deficit. To achieve this, external financial and speculative flows were regulated and there was equilibrium between exports and imports to stabilize the exchange rate.

In 1989, the Central Bank became autonomous and started an inflation reduction plan that was meant to be gradual, using an exchange rate band. It was abandoned in 1999 after the Asian crisis depreciated its currency and was replaced by an explicit target. In addition, the government adopted a fiscal policy consisting of savings during the high points of the economic cycle and a transparent government expenditure plan that stabilized prices and made the economy resilient to externals shocks (see Caputo and Saravia (2018)). At the present time, Chile has a reliable monetary policy, which includes inflation targeting and a floating exchange rate, prepared to mitigate exchanges risks, according to Corbo and Hernández (2005).

2.5 Colombia

At the beginning of the twentieth century, Colombia did not have a central bank in charge of the country's monetary policy. In 1960, the government nationalized a private and autonomous entity, the Banco de la República. In 1963, the monetary board was created and became responsible for Colombia's monetary policy. In the period 1960–70, inflation was relatively low, according to Perez-Reyna and

Osorio-Rodríguez (2016), as a result of the small size of the government. Nevertheless, 1963 was an exceptional year, mainly because the inflation rate reached 33.6 percent. Furthermore, in that period, the exchange rate changed to a controlled regime, and a strict control on all transactions in foreign currency was established. Until 1967, the year in which the new regime was established, there was export earnings instability and shortcomings in domestic policies, as explained in Jaramillo et al. (1999).

In 1974, the government initiated financial reform. The credit policy was restructured and the legal reserve requirement was reduced. Until the end of that decade, the recurrent use of the legal reserve requirement to confront the growth of currencies that came from the coffee boom not only caused unsustainable burdens for the financial system, but it also showed itself to be insufficient due to the magnitude of the international reserves shocks, according to Sánchez et al. (2005). In 1975, the coffee crisis in Brazil caused a sixfold increase in world prices. This led to devaluation of the peso from the existing exchange rate but did not change government policy according to Jaramillo et al. (1999).

Perez-Reyna and Osorio-Rodríguez (2016) explain that between 1975 and 1978, the coffee boom caused an appreciation of the peso by more than 20 percent. From 1977 until 1982, the size of the state grew by almost 50 percent. As a result of a financial crisis in 1982, banks were nationalized and the central bank financed loans for the productive sectors in the economy using monetary emissions.

By 1984, Colombia did not have the support of international financial institutions, making external credit sources unavailable without their intervention, as per Jaramillo et al. (1999). The Colombian government had the firm determination to avoid going to the International Monetary Fund (IMF). However, in 1984, the IMF and the Colombian government reached a monitoring agreement. The Colombian authorities wanted to have the "seal of approval" of the IMF (International Monetary Fund (2001)). And so, by the end of 1985, reserves began to increase and restrictions on imports were gradually reduced. Finally, relating to inflation, from 1971 to 1990, the average inflation rate increased to 23.1 percent.

By 1991, Colombia has promulgated a new political constitution, which included institutional reforms that affected the operating mechanism between fiscal and monetary policy. It also gave the central bank more independence. A board of governors replaced the monetary board. In this period, the government changed its foreign exchange rate policy as well, as it allowed foreign exchange rates to be partially determined by the market (see Perez-Reyna and Osorio-Rodríguez (2016)).

Colombia shifted from a crawling band to a flexible exchange rate regime in 1999, explains Chamon et al. (2019); since that time, the exchange rate has occasional interventions from the central bank to reduce volatility effects (see Perez-Reyna and Osorio-Rodríguez (2016)). Therefore, with a flexible exchange rate, monetary policy had the main objective of maintaining low inflation rates.

According to Perez-Reyna and Osorio-Rodríguez (2016), since 2000, Colombia has macroeconomic stability. The central bank began to adopt an inflation-targeting scheme by the beginning of 2001. The economy entered a long expansionary period, the result of a new institutional arrangement that established a ceiling on government debt. During the global crisis of 2008–9, it showed resilience to external shocks. However, according to a recent evaluation from the IMF,[2] the economy is in continuous exposure to extreme external shocks due to the importance of the oil sector and the high proportion of foreign investors in the local market of public debt.

2.6 Paraguay

As explained in Charotti et al. (2019), in the early 1950s, Paraguay was going through a critical economic situation, coupled with political instability and union pressure that demanded salary increases (Fernández Valdovinos and Monge Naranjo (2003)). In 1952, the Central Bank of Paraguay was created; among its functions were the purchase and sale of foreign currencies, currency issuance, re-discounting operations, and the orientation of the exchange and credit policies.

The Central Bank appears in the context of an unfavorable economic environment, with high inflation rates that extended from 1951 to 1954 – a consequence of an excessive increase in domestic prices and a devaluation of the guaraní (the Paraguayan currency). To cope with the monetary mismatch, in 1955 Gustavo Storm, president of the Central Bank, appealed to the IMF for an emergency loan. The fund, in addition to granting the credit line, sent a commission to Paraguay to prepare a plan for the financial adjustment of the country, according to Lara, Pankow, Insfrán, Caballero and Cantero (2013).

In 1956, the government initialized a stabilization plan in which the exchange rate was the policy instrument. Supported by this plan, inflation during the 1960s stayed below one digit. However, in the following decade, inflation started to rise and by 1974 inflation had reached 24 percent (see Charotti et al. (2019)).

---

[2] www.banrep.gov.co/es/noticias/comunicado-22–05-2019

The 1960s and 1970s saw Paraguay growing at a good pace (Lara, Pankow, Insfrán, Caballero and Cantero (2013), p. 16). The Itaipu hydroelectric dam was the main driver of growth in the 1970s. Its construction created an increase in effective demand, causing an excess, partially covered by an increase in imports. This situation, combined with a spike in oil prices, resulted in inflationary pressures. By the end of the decade, inflation had reached 28.2 percent. Those sectors that had grown the most thanks to Itaipu were the most affected by inflation, as explained by Fernández Valdovinos and Monge Naranjo (2003). The authors mentions that because of the economic policy that Paraguay was pursuing at that time, the country was not prepared for the resources that the Itaipu dam generated. The problem, they state, was that the resources generated were spent as if they were permanent.

In the early 1980s, foreign reserves started to decline. When construction of Itaipu came to an end, capital inflows decreased, and the economic activity began to slow down. Twin economic crises in Argentina and Brazil also contributed. This, too, was considered a signal that the fixed exchange rate policy could not be sustained, according to Charotti et al. (2019). Therefore, during 1982–3, the country suffered its first recession in thirty years (see Insfrán Pelozo (2003)).

In 1989, a *coup d'état* took place and one of the most long-lasting dictatorships in Latin America ended, bringing in the democratic era in Paraguay. The new authorities in charge changed the constitution in 1992 and the macroeconomic policy (see Charotti et al. (2019) and Fernández Valdovinos and Monge Naranjo (2003)). Their objective was to reduce macroeconomic imbalances, so measures were taken to reduce the fiscal deficit (Lara, Pankow, Insfrán, Caballero and Cantero (2013), p. 16).

The Paraguayan financial system went through a number of structural changes, explains Insfrán Pelozo (2003): liberalization of the economy, no foreign exchange rate controls, and unification of the multiple exchange rates, and the currency was allowed to float (see Fernández Valdovinos and Monge Naranjo (2003)). All these changes produced a high inflation rate (Lara, Pankow, Insfrán, Caballero and Cantero (2013), p. 16).

Nevertheless, this deregulation in the economy, as Insfrán Pelozo (2003) points out, was not accompanied with a supervision improvement. Meanwhile, interest rates remained high, and that stimulated a strong capital inflow to the Paraguayan economy (Lara, Pankow, Insfrán, Caballero and Cantero (2013), p. 16). As a consequence, a financial crisis ensued at the beginning of 1995. From 1991 to 2003, monetary policy was based on a monetary aggregates scheme (see Charotti et al. (2019)).

The financial crisis lasted into 1998 and is considered the worst financial crisis in Paraguayan history, according to Charotti et al. (2019). The government intervened (investigated on site) in more than 50 percent of banks and other financial institutions and almost all the financial institutions intervened were liquidated, as related by Insfrán Pelozo (2003). Charotti et al. (2019) mention that during the crisis, the government had to cover deposits to prevent a massive bank run, as there was no deposit guarantee scheme. The Central Bank, which conducted the monetary policy, designed an annual monetary program focused on the growth of M0 (coins and bills). Inflation levels remained moderate.

Eventually, the authorities started a process of rearrangement of monetary and financial policy. Two laws were enacted: one assigned the Central Bank the preservation and security of the stability of the currency value and the promotion efficiency and stability in the financial system; the second one provided a regulatory framework, much stricter than its predecessor, for financial institutions (Lara, Pankow, Insfrán, Caballero and Cantero (2013), p. 16).

In 2004, other structural reforms began to take form. The Central Bank initiated a migration to an inflation-targeting scheme. It started with a 5 percent target but with no explicit commitment. Since 2011, the Central Bank has formally begun the implementation of an inflation-targeting scheme. The objective is to achieve a low, stable, and predictable inflation (Lara, Pankow, Insfrán, Caballero and Cantero (2013), p. 16).

To summarize, Paraguay can be characterized as a stable economy. For more than seventy years, Paraguay has not experienced any hyperinflation episodes or any major macroeconomic imbalances. The guarani has been the local currency since 1943 and has not changed once, which is a major achievement in the region (Lara, Pankow, Insfrán, Caballero and Cantero (2013), p. 16).

2.7 Peru

First and foremost, it is important to mention that the creation process of the central bank and the beginnings of its currency are remarkably old (by Latin American standards). In 1863, after Senate approval, then-president San Román enacted the law that established the sol as the Peruvian currency (Dargent 2018).

In January 1922, the Congress received a proposal to create a central bank based on the US Federal Reserve Bank (the Fed). The idea to create a central bank in the country was by then two years old, and the Senate finally enacted Law 4500, which created the Reserve Bank of Peru (Dargent, 2018).

The Great Depression of the 1930s affected Peru because its debt was financed with export commodities to the United States. The crisis stopped imports from Peru, and a payment deficit was created; Peru experienced fiscal and exchange imbalances (Dargent, 2018).

According to Gozzi and Tappatá (2010), the Reserve Bank of Peru's president, Manuel Olaechea, proposed a mission led by Princeton economics professor Edwin Kemmerer in November 1930. The government then began important reforms, affecting economic policies, taxes, public credit, monetary regulation, and Reserve Bank's reorganization, with Kemmerer's advice. With his proposals, Law 7137 concerning the Reserve Central Bank was enacted in April 1931. This institution took over the Reserve Bank's functions, assets, and obligations. The Reserve Central Bank's main function was to keep a stable currency value and to provide the country, when necessary, with a liquid credit increase (see Gozzi and Tappatá (2010)). The Central Reserve Bank also had to provide flexibility in monetary circulation.

In the more modern history of Peru, the year 1967 saw the fixed exchange rate take the Peruvian economy into an inflationary period, an international reserves deficit, and the first devaluation in a long time (Martinelli and Vega (2019)). General Juan Velasco Alvarado took the presidency through a *coup d'état* in 1968. During his first years, incomes were stable and total expenditures went from 25 percent of GDP to 34 percent of GDP in 1974. In 1975, Peruvian exports decreased, and the government did not want to let the exchange rate float. At this time, a second *coup d'état* occurred, and the new regime changed the exchange rate policy: devaluations became persistent and scheduled. This exchange rate increases, in turn, generated inflationary pressures (Martinelli and Vega (2019)).

In 1983, inflation reached 100 percent and then-president Alan García executed an Emergency Plan between 1985 and 1986. The objective was to stop inflation through generalized price controls and a fixed exchange rate. The government also paid its external debt. These actions produced an economic recovery and manageable inflation levels (Martinelli and Vega (2019), p. 19). According to Dargent (2018), in 1985, the government changed the sol as a result of inflation, and the inti appeared. The inti equivalency was 1,000 soles and had a complex and frustrating history. In a period called "La Debacle" (The Debacle), when inflation was increasing so quickly that new bills were useless, the government authorized the emission of management checks to the banks. Finally, in 1990, the new sol appeared and is still the national currency.

In 1991, the most important achievement of the economic stabilization program, which was implemented in 1990, was the considerable reduction of inflation. In addition to the implementation of policies related to the stabilization program, in 1991, a set of structural reforms was carried out that would affect not only the level of inflation but also production in general and the labor market (National Institute of Statistics and Informatics (INEI) (2016)).

In 1992, productive activity was affected by the presence of the phenomenon called "El Niño," and there was an increase in the exchange rate in the last quarter of that year that put pressure on interest rates, with a recessionary effect on economic activity. From 1993 to 1995, privatizations were implemented to a greater extent, generating an increase in capital flows from abroad. In this period, it is important to point out that monetary and fiscal policy worked with more coordination. The growth of production and investment required significant purchases of inputs and capital goods, mainly for industry, as well as durable and non-durable consumer goods of foreign origin, which resulted in growth rates of imports, increasing the trade balance deficit (National Institute of Statistics and Informatics (INEI) (2016)).

In 1996, the current growing account deficit on the balance of payments of previous years forced the application of fiscal and monetary policies that aimed at attenuating the pace of expansion of domestic demand and reducing imports, which caused a contraction in investments. In 1997, inflation was reduced, based on a better control of fiscal imbalances, primary issuance, and exchange rate floating. GDP grew due to the recovery in investments.

From 1998 to 2000, the economy was affected by negative factors. The effects of El Niño, the interruption of short-term external financing to Peruvian banks as a result of the Asian and Russian crises (1998), and the fall in the terms of trade. These factors, together with the stagnation of the privatization process, affected investment, which was reflected in negative rates or weak GDP growth (National Institute of Statistics and Informatics (INEI) (2016), p. 20).

In 2000, the Peruvian economy grew 3.1 percent and the inflation rate stayed at 3.7 percent. The economy was recovering from the international financial crisis, but it suffered a slowdown in its productive activity due to internal political instability. However, an improvement in foreign accounts was achieved and the inflation target was met (Banco Central de la Reserva del Peru (2000)).

Between 2002 and 2013, Peru was one of the fastest-growing countries in Latin America. However, between 2014 and 2018, the economy started to slow down, and this lead to a temporary drop in private investments, lower tax revenues, and a decline in consumption (World Bank (2017)). However, Peru experienced one of the highest growth rates on average in the region, with a growth rate in average of 4.9 percent since 2000 to 2018.

3 Literature Review

Exchange rate forecasting models have been around for more than one hundred years now, and the literature on forecasting theory and applications is extensive, to say the least. Models such as PPP and UIP have been thoroughly analyzed time and again (see, for instance, Balassa (1964) for PPP, where we already find a review of the extensive literature on PPP in existence by then and dating all the way back to Cassel (1918b); the aforementioned Lothian and Wu (2011) paper gives an indication of the relevance the UIP model still has). As a matter of fact, according to Dimand and Gomez Betancourt (2012), the UIP concept dates all the way back to Fisher (1896), where it was first laid out. An analysis of deviations from the UIP condition (excess returns or the "predictable excess returns puzzle") can be found in Lewis (1994). Molodtsova and Papell (2009) find that the UIP condition does not hold in the short run (in line with our own results in this Element in Section 5), but they do find evidence in support of Taylor rule fundamentals for out-of-sample forecasting. In terms of PPP, Froot and Rogoff (1995) find that in the very long run (four years and longer), the model appears to predict exchange rate movements. A further development in the theory was the monetary model proposed by Frenkel (1976) and Mussa (1977). Around this time, Dornbusch (1976) proposed a sticky price (SP) model based on monetary fundamentals, and Frenkel (1979) further developed this framework by emphasizing the role of expectations. Furthermore, Frankel (1982) extended his monetary model by including current account balances – a development that was shared by Hooper and Morton (1982) and is known, in general, as the Hooper-Morton model. However, Meese and Rogoff (1983) wrote a seminal paper in which they argue that no exchange rate model can outperform a driftless random walk in out-of-sample forecasting (and where they show that the Hooper-Morton innovation did not produce statistically significant improvements). The impact of this paper cannot be underestimated, as every subsequent study that focuses on exchange rate forecasting has used it as the benchmark paper with which to compare results. The seemingly devastating results were eventually called into question or reconfirmed by the large number of papers that followed. Already in Froot and Thaler (1990), we find that the authors argue that rational and efficient markets cannot explain exchange rate movements. Since then, Mark (1995) has proposed that at longer horizons, a monetary fundamentals model could provide better out-of-sample forecasts. Around this time, Frankel and Rose (1994) produced a survey of the models with fundamentals used to predict floating exchange rates that found that monetary fundamentals helped forecast exchange rates in the long run. Chinn and Meese (1995) also find that structural models do not work well in the short run but error correction terms (ECTs) show stark improvement in the long run. However, fundamentals models have been subject to criticism by Kilian and Taylor (2003) and Faust et al. (2003): they argue that improvements occur only within a two-year window and disappear afterward. In fact, Faust et al. (2003) provide evidence that the results in Mark (1995) are not robust to using real-time data for long-run predictability. Interestingly, Kilian and Taylor (2003) find that ESTAR (Exponential Smooth Transition Auto-Regressive) models are helpful in explaining real exchange rate behavior. Gourinchas and Rey (2007) find that a measure of external imbalances (called *nxa*), defined as a linear combination of exports, imports, foreign assets, and liabilities, beats a random walk in out-of-sample forecasting both in the short and the long run (in essence, extending the Hooper and Morton idea that current account balances do matter). But as mentioned in the Introduction, there is a study, in this case Alquist and Chinn (2008), showing that *nxa* has limited success.

Also of interest to the present study is Barnett et al. (2005), a work that shows that the use of Divisia monetary aggregates (an alternative form of monetary aggregation) and the user cost price dramatically improves the forecasting power of structural models. In a similar vein, Ghosh and Bhadury (2018) show that Divisia monetary aggregates are powerful indicators of exchange rate movements for several economies. Many papers empirically tested these standard models for forecasting of exchange rates of the more relevant currency pairs. One example is Engel et al. (2007), where the authors argue in favor of macroeconomic fundamentals models for long-run predictions of exchange rate movements while warning that improvements may not hold for long windows. More specifically, this study is based on Engel and West (2005), where the authors develop a theorem in which they show that under certain conditions, fundamentals models imply a random walk–like behavior of exchange rates. Both studies suggest that exchange rates contain information about fundamentals as well, and the former views a random walk as the wrong benchmark model and suggests alternatives (we stick to the random walk, however, as it is the predominant benchmark model in the literature). Another example of the use of fundamentals models is Hsing and Sergi (2009), who analyzed the behavior of the USD/EUR using the PPP, the UIP, and two extended Mundell-Fleming models with several focuses, finding a number of policy implications. Evidence in favor of UIP can also be found in Clark and West (2006) with an adjusted version of mean squared prediction errors (MSPE) as the evaluating criterion.

In terms of model choice, Rossi (2013) explains how a number of studies have used single-equation models. Among them, Bacchetta et al. (2009) argue that sample size explains the Meese and Rogoff puzzle; taking a different angle, Ferraro et al. (2015) show that there is no relationship between oil prices and exchange rates neither on a monthly nor a quarterly basis. In our case, we use single-equation models that include an error correction. There are several instances of these as well (including Mark (1995)): Abhyankar et al. (2005) find success using error correction models with monetary fundamentals, but Berkowitz and Giorgianni (2001) do not find predictability at long horizons.

The impact of using a rolling window approach has been studied as well, for example, by West (1996). It should be noted that discrepancies exist in in-sample and out-of-sample sizes, as pointed out by Rossi and Inoue (2012), where the authors discuss the instability of forecasting power of different models in different window sizes. Forecasting window sizes range from 49 in Chinn (1991) to 128 in Van Dijk and Franses (2003), depending also on the size of the total sample. Our case in this Element is closer to the latter work.

In terms of BMA, the combination of models with large data sets is at the heart of the model. Several authors have had some success in forecasting using large data sets as in Stock and Watson (2002) for the Index of Industrial Production, and Bernanke and Boivin (2003) for inflation. Moreover, Stock and Watson (2004) have used the combination of forecast methods to approximate output growth with encouraging results.[3] It is worth noting that forecast combination methods date back to Bates and Granger (1969).

BMA itself was first introduced by Leamer (1978) and was further developed by Raftery et al. (1997) and Hoeting et al. (1999). BMA was first used for exchange rate forecasting by Wright (2008) and subsequently by Lam et al. (2008). Both papers find that BMA produces improvements in out-of-sample forecasts when compared with a driftless random walk, especially in the short run. Neither paper tests for statistical significance of these improvements, though.

BVAR was used in forecasting as far back as Litterman (1986). Sarantis (2006) shows that a BVAR model outperforms a random walk in forecasting daily exchange rates. Banbura et al. (2007) use BVAR for forecasting employment, the consumer price index (CPI) and the federal funds rate with positive results for first-quarter predictions. In a similar fashion, Edge et al. (2010) use several BVAR specifications to forecast macroeconomic variables within a DSGE framework, while comparing the accuracy of the forecasts produced by their model to a benchmark model (the FRB/US model). Recently, Schüssler et al. (2018) have used VAR-based models with Bayesian estimation methods for exchange rate forecasting with some success.

A very thorough and comprehensive review of the more recent literature and methodology appears in the aforementioned Rossi (2013), where the author goes over many of the models that have been used in the past, the papers where they were used, the many methodologies and approaches, and the results produced. In the application, the author finds that Taylor rule fundamentals or net foreign assets are the best predictors, for the most part, when models are linear. The paper does not, however, deal with exchange rates from emerging

---

[3] Bernanke and Boivin (2003) also utilize forecast combination for inflation measures.

markets. In a similar vein, another study of interest is Wieland and Wolters (2013), where the authors describe different forecasting models for several macroeconomic variables used by central banks and policy makers, and their decision-making interactions with the resulting forecasts.

4 Methodology

In this section, we discuss the five models that we have used to estimate the different exchange rate forecasts under consideration and their respective specifications. Regarding the choice of the models, we followed Lam et al. (2008) and, partly, Cheung et al. (2019). In the final Section 4.6, we discuss how the assessment of the performance of each model is done.

4.1 Purchasing Power Parity

As mentioned in the previous section, PPP is a well-known and widely discussed theoretical model that gives a clear and intuitive explanation for exchange rate determination. The PPP model is expressed in the following manner:

$$\ln e_t = \ln p_t - \ln p_t^* \tag{1}$$

where e_t is the nominal exchange rate, p_t is the domestic price, and p_t^* is the foreign price.

The PPP specification used in this work follows Lam et al. (2008). This involves an error correction restriction and no short-run dynamics. What this means is that the variation from the exchange rate is a correction of the deviation from a long-run equilibrium in the previous period. And so, the form of the equation is

$$\ln e_{t+h} - \ln e_t = \alpha_0 + \alpha_1(\ln e_t - \beta_0 - \beta_1 \ln \tilde{p}_t) + \epsilon_t \tag{2}$$

where $\tilde{p}_t$ is the relative price level of the domestic economy relative to the foreign one, h is the forecast horizon, and ϵ_t is the error term.

4.2 Uncovered Interest-rate Parity

UIP is another model that has been studied repeatedly as an approximation to forecasting exchange rates. This model entails the no-arbitrage condition that the expected return of the exchange rate h periods ahead is equal to the interest rate differential, which can be expressed as

$$E_t(\ln e_{t+h} - \ln e_t) = i_t - i_t^* \tag{3}$$

where $E_t(\cdot)$ is the expectation at time t, and i_t and i_t^* are the domestic and foreign interest rates, respectively.

In a similar specification as the earlier one for the PPP model, also including an error correction restriction, we write the equation as

$$\ln e_{t+h} - \ln e_t = \alpha_0 + \alpha_1 \left(\ln e_t - \beta_0 - \beta_1 \ln \tilde{\imath}_t \right) + \epsilon_t \tag{4}$$

where $\tilde{\imath}_t$ is the relative interest rate (domestic to foreign).

4.3 Sticky Price

As in Frankel (1979), we can expand the PPP framework so that exchange rates are also determined by money supply, output, and interest rates. This is given by the following equation:

$$\ln e_t = \ln m_t - \ln m_t^* - \phi\left(\ln y_t - \ln y_t^*\right) + \lambda\left(\ln i_t - \ln i_t^*\right)$$
$$+ \beta\left(\ln \pi_t - \ln \pi_t^*\right) \tag{5}$$

where m_t and m_t^*, y_t and y_t^*, i_t and i_t^*, and π_t and π_t^*, are, respectively, domestic and foreign money supply, domestic and foreign output, domestic and foreign interest rates, and domestic and foreign current long-run expected rates of inflation.

As in the previous cases, we use a restrictive error correction form of the model:

$$\ln e_{t+h} - \ln e_t = \alpha_0 + \alpha_1 (\ln e_t - \beta_0 - \beta_1 \ln \tilde{m}_t - \beta_2 \ln \tilde{y}_t$$
$$- \beta_3 \ln \tilde{\imath}_t - \beta_4 \ln \tilde{p}_t) + \epsilon_t \tag{6}$$

where $\tilde{m}_t$, $\tilde{y}_t$, and $\tilde{\imath}_t$ are domestic to foreign relative money demand and output and short-term interest rates, respectively. Notice that we have replaced long-run expected rates of inflation with the only proxy available – relative prices. The reason for this choice will be explained in the next section.

4.4 Bayesian Model Averaging (BMA)

BMA is a forecasting method that utilizes large data sets and many different models. Say there are M_i models, indexed by $i = 1, 2, \ldots, n$, each of which θ_i. We do not know which model is the true model, but we assume that one of them is. We assume, then, that the i-th model is the true model based on some prior belief $P(M_i)$. The posterior probabilities are computed starting from a prior about which model is the true one. Thus, if D is the available data, the posterior probability that the i-th model is the true model is given by

$$P(M_i|D) = \frac{P(D|M_i)P(M_i)}{\sum_{j=1}^{n} P(D|M_j)P(M_j)} \tag{7}$$

where

$$P(D|M_i) = \int P(D|\theta_i, M_i)P(\theta_i|M_i)d\theta_i \tag{8}$$

$P(D|M_i)$ being the marginal likelihood for the model M_i; $P(\theta_i|M_i)$ is the prior density of the parameters and the likelihood is given by $P(D|\theta_i, M_i)$.[4] The forecasts from each of the different models are then weighted by their respective posteriors. The model is assumed to be linear. And so, one has

$$y = X_i\beta_i + \epsilon \tag{9}$$

where y is the vector of exchange rates (in this case), X_i are the predictors, β_i are parameters, ϵ is an i.i.d. error with mean zero and variance σ^2 and $\theta_i = (\beta_i', \sigma^2)$. We also assume that the regressors are strictly exogenous. As Wright (2008) argues, even when dealing with time series, it is possible to make this assumption and still have good forecasting power.

As for the coefficients, we assume a prior mean of zero. The structure of their variance is given by Zellner's g so that

$$\beta_i \Big| g \sim N\left(0, \sigma^2 \left(\frac{1}{gX_i'X_i}\right)^{-1}\right) \tag{10}$$

where the hyper-parameter g is set to the default "unit information prior" $g = n$ (the number of models).

The forecasting model is then given by

$$\ln e_{t+h} - \ln e_t = \beta_i' X_{i,t} + \epsilon_t \tag{11}$$

where $X_{i,t}$ is the vector of regressors at time t for model i. For each model, we have a forecast $\tilde{\beta}_i' X_{i,t}$ where $\tilde{\beta}_i'$ is the posterior mean of β_i. Each model is weighted by its posterior probabilities so that the forecast is given by $\sum_{i=1}^{n} P(M_i|D)\tilde{\beta}_i' X_{i,t}$ where $P(M_i|D)$ is the posterior probability of the i-th model and D is the data set.

---

[4] Wright (2008) discusses the distinction between model uncertainty and parameter uncertainty.

4.5 Bayesian Vector Autoregression (BVAR)

Litterman (1986) introduced the BVAR model with a Minnesota prior. As previously described, it has been widely used in forecasting. If the model is as follows:

$$y = (I_m \otimes X)a + \epsilon, \quad \epsilon \sim (0, \Sigma_\epsilon \otimes I_T) \tag{12}$$

then y and ϵ are $mT \times 1$ are vectors of dependent variables and errors, respectively, and where m is the number of variables and T, the time periods. I_m is the identity matrix, X is the matrix of independent variables, and α is a $ml \times 1$ vector where l is the number of lags. More specifically, $\alpha = \bar{a} + \xi_\alpha$ with $\xi_\alpha \sim N(0, \Sigma_\alpha)$, where in the Minnesota prior $\bar{a} = 0$ except $\overline{a_{1i}} = 1, i = 1, , m$, Σ_α is diagonal and each element $\alpha_{ij,l}$ (equation i, variable j, and lag l) is as follows

$$\sigma_{ij,l} = \phi_0/h(l), \quad i = j \tag{13}$$

If j is endogenous, then

$$\sigma_{ij,l} = \phi_0 \times \phi_1/h(l) \times (\sigma_j/\sigma_i)^2, \quad i \neq j \tag{14}$$

And if j is exogenous, then

$$\sigma_{ij,l} = \phi_0 \times \phi_2 \tag{15}$$

In this case $\phi_0, \phi_1, \phi_2, (\sigma_j/\sigma_i)^2$ and $h(l)$ are, respectively, hyper-parameters, a scaling factor, and a function of lags l. Note that ϕ_0 measures the tightness of the first lag's variance, ϕ_1 is the relative tightness of any other variables, and ϕ_2 is the relative tightness of exogenous variables. Finally, $h(l)$ is a measure of the relative tightness of the variance of the lags.

The error correction model follows a similar process to the one laid out for the SP model, using the same variables. The number of lags is 1.

4.6 Out-of-sample Performance Evaluation: Root Mean Square Error Ratio and Direction of Change

In order to evaluate our models out-of-sample (OOS), we use the recursive window approach. Given our division of in-sample (IS) and out-of-sample (OOS) periods, we use our IS data to start the recursive estimation, in this approach at each $t \in \tau_{OOS}$, where τ_{OOS} represents the OOS subset of the entire sample. We use all the available information from the set of predictors ranging from the first observation in-sample up to t to form the matrix $X_{i,t}$ to forecast h periods ahead of t this being the variation of the log of the exchange rate. With the fitted model at t, we can obtain the residuals for each framework. This procedure is repeated in next period $t+1$, updating the estimated coefficient and obtaining the residuals, until the end of all the OOS observations.

To evaluate the accuracy of each model in the OOS period, we compare each one to a benchmark model, which in this case is the driftless random walk given by

$$\ln e_{t+h} - \ln e_t = \epsilon_t \tag{16}$$

Following the Meese and Rogoff (1983) methodology, we take the expectation of the random walk so that it becomes a martingale process. In other words, the predictor of the exchange rate h periods ahead is whatever the exchange rate is at time t. This is, in more precise terms, what we refer to when we say that our benchmark model is the random walk.

First, we start the evaluation process with the root mean square error (RMSE) of each of the models by dividing them by the RMSE from the random walk. This is also known as Theil's U statistic, as Theil (1971) introduced it. Using this statistic allows us to interpret this ratio as to how the OOS RMSE generated by each model compares to the OOS RMSE of a simulated random walk. A ratio of less than one indicates that the model is performing better than the random walk and vice versa. This loss function is the standard choice in the majority of works that deal with exchange rate forecasting when it comes to the evaluation of performance, as can be seen in Rossi (2013). We assess the OOS performance of each model considering four horizons $h = 3, 6, 9$, and 12 months ahead.

We also evaluate the direction of change (DoC) ratio. This statistic is very common as an alternative when evaluating the forecasting power of any model, as in Engel (1994) and Cerra and Saxena (2010). The DoC measures the proportion of times each model correctly predicts actual exchange rate increases or decreases (that is, the direction of change). Assuming that the expected value of random walk predicting the right direction of change is 0.5, values higher than 0.5 indicate that a model is outperforming the random walk and values lower than 0.5 indicate the opposite. The higher the proportion is, the better the model is performing.

The third method is the statistic produced by Diebold and Mariano (1995), which allows for the comparison of forecasts in terms of whether the difference between two forecasts for the same forecasting period is statistically significant and whether the improvement is statistically significant (and thus, one forecast is "better" than another). If $g(e_{it})$ is the loss function of a forecast error (the difference between the actual exchange rate and forecast, squared), the loss differential function is defined as $d_t = g(e_{1t}) - g(e_{2t})$. If d_t is zero, then the forecasts under examination are equally accurate. Under the null, the expected value of d_t is zero. The DM statistic itself takes the form

$$DM = \frac{\bar{d}}{\sqrt{2\pi \hat{f}_d(0)/T}} \qquad (17)$$

where $\bar{d}$ is the sample mean of the loss differential function, and $\hat{f}_d(0)$ is a consistent estimate of the spectral density. Under the null, $DM \to N(0,1)$. The null is rejected if $|DM| > z_{\alpha/2}$.

5 Data

The data for this Element are monthly series of the bilateral exchange rates between the Argentinian peso and the United States dollar (ARS/USD), the Brazilian real and the United States dollar (BRL/USD), the Bolivian peso and the United States dollar (BOB/USD), the Chilean peso and the United States dollar (CLP/USD), the Colombian peso and the United States dollar (COP/USD), the Peruvian sol against the United States dollar (PEN/USD), the Paraguayan guarani against the United States dollar (PYG/USD), the Paraguayan guarani against the Brazilian real (PYG/BRL), and the Paraguayan guarani against the Argentinian peso (PYG/ARS). These series start and finish as follows: from January 1997 to June 2017 for the ARS/USD exchange rate, from January 2006 to October 2016 for the BOB/USD exchange rate, from January 1994 to June 2017 for the BRL/USD exchange rate, from February 1997 to June 2017 for the CLP/USD exchange rate, from January 2005 to December 2014 for the COP/USD exchange rate, from January 2001 to June 2017 for the PEN/USD exchange rate, from January 1994 to June 2017 for the PYG/USD exchange rate, from January 1994 to June 2017 for the PYG/BRL exchange rate, and from January 1997 to June 2017 for the PYG/ARS exchange rate. The reason we chose to start the series at these particular dates is due mainly to the use of monthly economic activity indexes as proxies for output. None of the countries evaluated, except for the United States, keeps a monthly GDP statistic. It turned out that several of them maintained these economic activity indexes for a limited time and then either dropped them or no longer made them available, as in the case of Bolivia and Colombia. Another problem in terms of data availability was that Paraguay, for instance, had no record of monthly exchange rates with any country before January 1994. The lack of data was also the reason why we could not take Uruguay into account: neither its central bank nor its statistics institute keeps a monthly measure of economic activity. The case of Venezuela is far more complicated, since in its data are missing for long periods, and it is actually not deemed trustworthy by the International

Monetary Fund (IMF).[5] On the other hand, data availability was not the issue with Ecuador, but the fact that its economy is fully dollarized.

The choice of IS and OOS data was based on the conclusion of the of the 2008–9 housing crisis, known commonly as the Great Recession. Because most exchange rates are against the dollar, and for consistency, the IS period for all countries runs from whenever the series begin to the second quarter of 2009 and the OOS from then until the end of each series.

For BMA, following Wright (2008) and Lam et al. (2008), we consider the following monthly variables as potential predictors: (1) short-term interest rates and relative short-term interest rates, (2) log of output and log of relative output (domestic to foreign), (3) log of money supply and log of relative money supply (domestic to foreign), (4) log of price levels and log of relative price levels (domestic to foreign), (5) oil price, and for the particular case of each country, (6) main export. This gives a total of 2^6 possible models.

The choice of interest rates for the SP and UIP models varies from country to country and was done not only following Frankel's methodology or by choice but also out of necessity – sometimes these were the only interest rates that had been consistently reported since the start of each series. We should then specify what these interest rates are: the monetary policy rate for Argentina, the inter-bank lending rate for Bolivia, the monetary policy rate for Brazil, the monetary policy rate for Chile, the monetary policy rate for Colombia, the monetary policy rate for Peru, the short-term interest rate on deposits for Paraguay, and, the federal funds rate for the United States. On a similar note, the choice of consumer price index (CPI) as a proxy for expected inflation was also done following Frankel and out of necessity: of all the possible proxies used by Frankel, it was the only one available. The proxies for monthly output were the Monthly Estimator of Economic Activity (EMAE) produced by the National Institute of Statistics and Census (INDEC) for Argentina; the monthly Global Economic Activity Index (IGAE) produced by the National Institute of Statistics (INE) for Bolivia; the index of monthly monetary activity (IBC-Br) produced by the Central Bank of Brazil (BCB) for Brazil; the Monthly Economic Activity Index (IMACEC) produced by the Central Bank of Chile (BCC); the Monthly Economic Activity Index in Colombia (IMACO) produced by the central bank of Colombia, the Bank of the Republic; and the Monthly Economic Activity Index (IMAEP) produced by the Central Bank of Paraguay (BCP). All these indexes track the performance of the most relevant industries in each country. Finally, main exports were included in the BMA model because they represent a significant portion of

[5] See for instance Reuters. *IMF denies pressuring Venezuela to release economic data* at www .reuters.com/article/us-venezuela-politics-imf/imf-denies-pressuring-venezuela-to-release-eco nomic-data-idUSKCN1T01YW

each of these countries GDPs. Also, the soy, oil, and copper markets are highly dollarized. All the Bolivian data were retrieved from the Central Bank of Bolivia except the IGAE. The Brazilian data were taken from the BCB statistical bulletin, except the CPI, which was retrieved from the Getulio Vargas Foundation website. All the Chilean data were taken from the BCC website. All the Colombian data were taken from the Bank of the Republic website. All the Peruvian data were retrieved from the Central Bank of the Republic of Peru's (BCRP) website. All the data pertaining to Paraguay, as well as oil and soy prices, were obtained from the Statistical Annex of the yearly Economic Report published by the BCP. M1 monetary aggregates, CPI, and three-month Treasury bill interest rates for the United States were retrieved from the Federal Reserve Bank of Saint Louis's Federal Reserve Economic Data (FRED). US monthly GDP data were obtained from the Macroeconomic Advisers data bank.

For the Argentinian data, an observation should be made. Its M1 aggregates were taken from the FRED, and interest rates from the Central Bank of the Argentine Republic's (BCRA) site. But the CPI had to be constructed from four sources: the original CPI series from INDEC (base year 2008), a second CPI series from INDEC (base year 2014), a third CPI series from INDEC (base year 2016), and a parallel series put together by the Argentine Congress, as the INDEC stopped producing its CPI series from November 2015 to November 2016. This series was retrieved from Ambito.com, the internet website that compiled it.

6 Results

6.1 Coefficients in the PPP and UIP Models

Before discussing the results, Figures 1, 2, and 3 depict the behavior of the coefficients for the PPP and UIP models in the first regression of the error correction. As might be expected, they almost always differ from 1. The aforementioned paper by Froot and Thaler (1990) also mentions that the β coefficient in UIP is almost never equal to 1. This, the authors explain, is usually associated in the literature with a time-varying risk premium or expectational errors on the part of agents. This means that any 1 percent increase in the interest rate differential would imply a less than 1 percent decrease in the value of the home currency. If β is smaller than 0, then an increase in the interest rate differential implies a decrease in expected depreciation, meaning expected depreciation and risk premia have a negative covariance. The authors make no mention of what a β greater than 1 implies, as this is never observed in general (and neither is it observed in this study).

What all of this does is underscore the need to adjust the models by using an error-correcting approach, as these relations are clearly not stable across time and can vary greatly from model to model and from case to case.

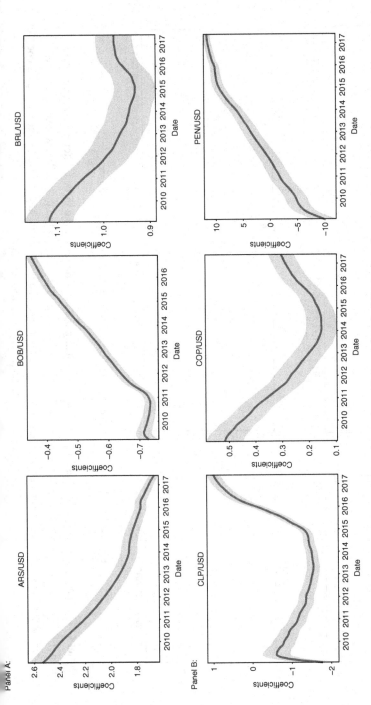

Figure 1 PPP estimated coefficients for six bilateral exchange rates

Panel A This panel reports the OOS estimated coefficients using the PPP model for the three bilateral exchange rates.
Panel B This panel reports the OOS estimated coefficients using the PPP model for the three bilateral exchange rates.
For each plot in both panels, the x-axis represents the OOS t in the recursive window approach, and the y-axis the estimated coefficients.
Shaded areas denote 68 percent confidence bands.

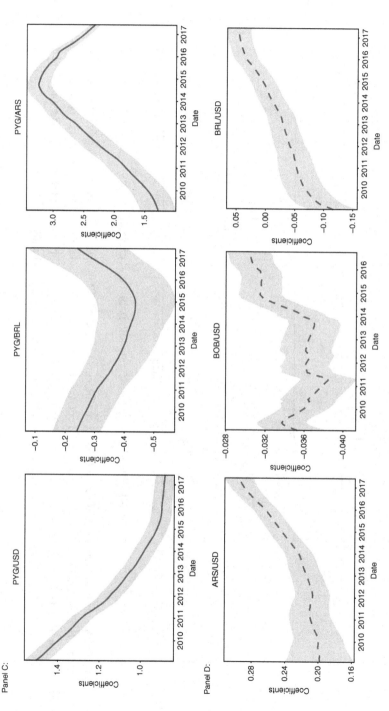

Figure 2 PPP and UIP estimated coefficients for six bilateral exchange rates

Panel C This panel reports the OOS estimated coefficients using the PPP model for the three bilateral exchange rates.
Panel D This panel reports the OOS estimated coefficients using the UIP model for the three bilateral exchange rates.
For each plot in both panels, the x-axis represents the OOS t in the recursive window approach, and the y-axis the estimated coefficients.
Shaded areas denote 68 percent confidence bands.

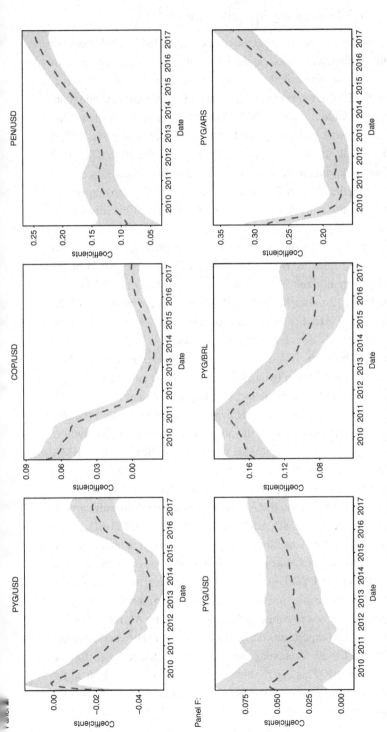

Figure 3 UIP estimated coefficients for six bilateral exchange rates

Panel E This panel reports the OOS estimated coefficients using the UIP model for the three bilateral exchange rates.

Panel F This panel reports the OOS estimated coefficients using UIP model for the three bilateral exchange rates for Paraguay.

For each plot in both panels, the x-axis represents the OOS t in the recursive window approach, and the y-axis the estimated coefficients. Shaded areas denote 68 percent confidence bands.

6.2 Comparing Models Using RMSE

As discussed in Section 4, we are using the ratio of the RMSE of each model to the RMSE of the random walk to assess their performance. Recall that a ratio of less than 1 is an improvement over the random walk, and vice versa. Tables 1, 2, 3, 4, and 5 show the RMSE ratios of the nine exchange rates under examination.

As can be seen in Table 1, panel A, PPP produces better forecasts in the long run in four out of the nine exchange rates. For the ARS/USD and PYG/ARS, it beats the random walk in every forecasting horizon. For the BRL/USD, PPP beats the random walk in three periods (6, 9, and 12 months ahead). In the 12-month-head horizon, the PYG/BRL forecasts produced by PPP also outperform the random walk. In the other five cases, the random walk still predicts more accurately in every horizon.

In Table 2, panel A, UIP produces better forecasts in the long run in four out of the nine exchange rates as well. These UIP-produced forecasts beat the random walk in every horizon in the case of the ARS/USD and PYG/USD exchange rates. In the 12-month horizon, UIP outperforms the random walk for BRL/USD and PYG/BRL. For all other exchange rates and for all other horizons, the random walk does better than the model.

Table 3, panel A, shows the RMSE ratios for the SP model. Its forecasts beat those of the random walk only in two cases: the ARS/USD and the PYG/ARS exchange rates. In the first case, SP does exceedingly well, and in both cases, forecasts improve in the later horizons. However, the random walk produces better forecasts for every period for all the other exchange rates under study.

Panel A in Table 4 displays the RMSE ratios for the BMA model. BMA outperforms the random walk in the short run and loses forecasting power as we get past the 6-month horizon (the RMSE ratios become larger in most cases). In six out of the nine exchange rates, BMA outperforms the random walk, producing better forecasts for ARS/USD, BRL/USD, COP/USD, PEN/USD, PYG/USD, and PYG/BRL in the 3-month horizon. In the 6-months ahead period, forecasts are better for six exchange rates as well – the same ones, except now PYG/ARS does better but PYG/USD does not. For the last two horizons, the same six forecast exchange rates are better than the random walk.

In Table 5, panel A, we observe the RMSE ratios for the BVAR model. Under this criterion, this model outperforms the random walk for all currencies (except the BOB/USD) and for all forecasting horizons, except the last two for the PYG/USD exchange rate. This clearly breaks the pattern we have seen so far with all other models, since none of them beats the random walk so consistently across exchange rates and periods.

Table 1 PPP: Ratio of PPP RMSE, RMSE and DoC

Panel A: Ratio of Models RMSE over Random Walk RMSE

	3 months	6 months	9 months	12 months
ARS/USD	0.864	0.754	0.674	0.609
BOB/USD	3.432	5.329	6.969	7.524
BRL/USD	1.002	0.978	0.938	0.892
CLP/USD	1.034	1.087	1.084	1.046
COP/USD	1.030	1.118	1.170	1.125
PEN/USD	1.078	1.251	1.361	1.407
PYG/USD	1.000	1.028	1.060	1.095
PYG/BRL	0.994	1.052	1.044	0.974
PYG/ARS	0.937	0.900	0.864	0.804

Panel B: Root Mean Square Error (RMSE)

	3 months	6 months	9 months	12 months
ARS/USD	0.005	0.011	0.017	0.023
BOB/USD	0.000	0.000	0.001	0.001
BRL/USD	0.006	0.014	0.022	0.028
CLP/USD	0.002	0.005	0.008	0.011
COP/USD	0.005	0.012	0.021	0.029
PEN/USD	0.008	0.031	0.069	0.120
PYG/USD	0.003	0.007	0.010	0.013
PYG/BRL	0.008	0.023	0.040	0.050
PYG/ARS	0.008	0.017	0.028	0.035

Panel C: DoC

	3 months	6 months	9 months	12 months
ARS/USD	0.857	0.842	0.859	0.899
BOB/USD	0.594	0.557	0.565	0.537
BRL/USD	0.510	0.611	0.467	0.517
CLP/USD	0.490	0.600	0.609	0.573
COP/USD	0.490	0.537	0.478	0.517
PEN/USD	0.888	0.853	0.880	0.888
PYG/USD	0.490	0.411	0.522	0.539
PYG/BRL	0.531	0.568	0.587	0.618
PYG/ARS	0.490	0.537	0.533	0.607

Table 1 summarizes the out-of-sample (OOS) ratio of the PPP RMSE over the random walk RMSE, its RMSE, and its DoC. The exchange rates assessed are ARS/USD, BOB/USD, BLR/USD, CLP/USD, COP/USD, PEN/USD, PYG/USD, PYG/BRL, and PYG/ARS. Panel A reports the RMSE ratios, panel B reports the RMSEs, and panel C reports the DoC ratios. The table summarizes the result for four horizons: $h = 3, 6, 9,$ and 12 months. Under the RMSE criterion, a number lower than 1 means that the model in the row predicts better than the random walk benchmark. Under the DoC criterion, a ratio greater than 0.5 indicates that the model is outperforming the random walk.

Table 2 UIP: Ratio of UIP RMSE, RMSE and DoC

Panel A: Ratio of Model RMSE over Random Walk RMSE

	3 months	6 months	9 months	12 months
ARS/USD	0.922	0.924	0.902	0.859
BOB/USD	2.926	3.621	4.333	4.388
BRL/USD	1.138	1.082	1.011	0.980
CLP/USD	1.063	1.142	1.166	1.139
COP/USD	1.028	1.104	1.133	1.087
PEN/USD	1.092	1.288	1.396	1.413
PYG/USD	0.990	0.974	0.955	0.932
PYG/BRL	0.976	1.021	1.009	0.934
PYG/ARS	0.966	1.058	1.081	1.030

Panel B: Root Mean Square Error (RMSE)

	3 months	6 months	9 months	12 months
ARS/USD	0.006	0.017	0.030	0.045
BOB/USD	0.000	0.000	0.000	0.000
BRL/USD	0.008	0.017	0.026	0.034
CLP/USD	0.002	0.005	0.009	0.013
COP/USD	0.005	0.012	0.020	0.027
PEN/USD	0.009	0.033	0.073	0.121
PYG/USD	0.003	0.006	0.008	0.009
PYG/BRL	0.008	0.022	0.037	0.046
PYG/ARS	0.008	0.024	0.043	0.057

Panel C: DoC

	3 months	6 months	9 months	12 months
ARS/USD	0.847	0.768	0.793	0.787
BOB/USD	0.561	0.443	0.435	0.426
BRL/USD	0.510	0.621	0.478	0.517
CLP/USD	0.480	0.611	0.587	0.539
COP/USD	0.480	0.537	0.554	0.551
PEN/USD	0.827	0.779	0.696	0.652
PYG/USD	0.490	0.411	0.489	0.539
PYG/BRL	0.531	0.547	0.554	0.584
PYG/ARS	0.500	0.526	0.457	0.573

Table 2 summarizes the out-of-sample (OOS) ratio of the UIP RMSE over the random walk RMSE, its RMSE, and its DoC. The exchange rates assessed are- ARS/USD, BOB/USD, BLR/USD, CLP/USD, COP/USD, PEN/USD, PYG/USD, PYG/BRL, and PYG/ARS. Panel A reports the RMSE ratios, panel B reports the RMSEs, and panel C reports de DoC ratios. The table summarizes the result for four horizons: $h = 3, 6, 9$, and 12 months. Under the RMSE criterion, a number lower than 1 means that the model in the row predicts better than the random walk benchmark. Under the DoC criterion, a ratio greater than 0.5 indicates that the model is outperforming the random walk.

Table 3 SP: Ratio of SP RMSE, RMSE and DoC

Panel A: Ratio of Models RMSE over Random Walk RMSE

	3 months	6 months	9 months	12 months
ARS/USD	0.837	0.879	0.802	0.647
BOB/USD	4.032	5.879	7.451	7.842
BRL/USD	1.132	1.132	1.127	1.115
CLP/USD	1.099	1.188	1.198	1.160
COP/USD	1.118	1.245	1.284	1.203
PEN/USD	1.095	1.298	1.435	1.470
PYG/USD	1.017	1.042	1.067	1.092
PYG/BRL	1.107	1.210	1.214	1.170
PYG/ARS	0.983	0.909	0.853	0.804

Panel B: Root Mean Square Error (RMSE)

	3 months	6 months	9 months	12 months
ARS/USD	0.005	0.015	0.024	0.025
BOB/USD	0.000	0.000	0.001	0.002
BRL/USD	0.008	0.019	0.032	0.044
CLP/USD	0.003	0.006	0.010	0.013
COP/USD	0.006	0.015	0.025	0.034
PEN/USD	0.009	0.033	0.077	0.131
PYG/USD	0.003	0.007	0.010	0.013
PYG/BRL	0.010	0.031	0.054	0.072
PYG/ARS	0.009	0.018	0.027	0.035

Panel C: DoC

	3 months	6 months	9 months	12 months
ARS/USD	0.765	0.642	0.587	0.596
BOB/USD	0.606	0.477	0.470	0.340
BRL/USD	0.551	0.600	0.500	0.494
CLP/USD	0.469	0.642	0.522	0.449
COP/USD	0.561	0.568	0.500	0.449
PEN/USD	0.724	0.621	0.641	0.618
PYG/USD	0.480	0.421	0.511	0.596
PYG/BRL	0.520	0.579	0.489	0.551
PYG/ARS	0.480	0.547	0.489	0.607

Table 3 summarizes the out-of-sample (OOS) ratio of the SP RMSE over the random walk RMSE, its RMSE, and its DoC. The exchange rates assessed are ARS/USD, BOB/USD, BLR/USD, CLP/USD, COP/USD, PEN/USD, PYG/USD, PYG/BRL, and PYG/ARS. Panel A reports the RMSE ratios, panel B reports the RMSEs, and panel C reports the DoC ratios. The table summarizes the result for four horizons: $h = 3, 6, 9,$ and 12 months. Under the RMSE criterion, a number lower than 1 means that the model in the row predicts better than the random walk benchmark. Under the DoC criterion, a ratio greater than 0.5 indicates that the model is outperforming the random walk.

Table 4 BMA: Ratio of BMA RMSE, RMSE and DoC

Panel A: Ratio of Models RMSE over Random Walk RMSE

	3 months	6 months	9 months	12 months
ARS/USD	0.910	0.795	0.799	0.816
BOB/USD	2.024	1.702	1.646	1.537
BRL/USD	0.945	0.952	0.992	0.991
CLP/USD	1.013	1.037	1.022	1.044
COP/USD	0.767	0.853	0.879	0.879
PEN/USD	0.931	0.889	0.894	0.904
PYG/USD	⋅ 0.935	1.005	1.058	1.059
PYG/BRL	0.882	0.907	0.916	0.915
PYG/ARS	1.000	0.913	0.906	0.897

Panel B: Root Mean Square Error (RMSE)

	3 months	6 months	9 months	12 months
ARS/USD	0.006	0.012	0.024	0.040
BOB/USD	0.000	0.000	0.000	0.000
BRL/USD	0.005	0.013	0.025	0.035
CLP/USD	0.002	0.004	0.007	0.011
COP/USD	0.003	0.007	0.012	0.018
PEN/USD	0.006	0.016	0.030	0.050
PYG/USD	0.002	0.006	0.010	0.012
PYG/BRL	0.007	0.017	0.031	0.044
PYG/ARS	0.009	0.018	0.030	0.043

Panel C: DoC

	3 months	6 months	9 months	12 months
ARS/USD	0.694	0.632	0.620	0.663
BOB/USD	0.583	0.546	0.554	0.549
BRL/USD	0.541	0.537	0.413	0.528
CLP/USD	0.571	0.589	0.609	0.528
COP/USD	0.582	0.579	0.554	0.539
PEN/USD	0.714	0.726	0.728	0.764
PYG/USD	0.571	0.463	0.424	0.494
PYG/BRL	0.571	0.568	0.533	0.674
PYG/ARS	0.531	0.537	0.489	0.562

Table 4 summarizes the out-of-sample (OOS) ratio of the BMA RMSE over the random walk RMSE, its RMSE, and its DoC. The exchange rates assessed are- ARS/USD, BOB/USD, BLR/USD, CLP/USD, COP/USD, PEN/USD, PYG/USD, PYG/BRL, and PYG/ARS. Panel A reports the RMSE ratios, panel B reports the RMSEs, and panel C reports the DoC ratios. The table summarizes the result for four horizons: $h = 3, 6, 9,$ and 12 months. Under the RMSE criterion, a number lower than 1 means that the model in the row predicts better than the random walk benchmark. Under the DoC criterion, a ratio greater than 0.5 indicates that the model is outperforming the random walk.

Table 5 BVAR: Ratio of BVAR RMSE, RMSE and DoC

Panel A: Ratio of Models RMSE over Random Walk RMSE

	3 months	6 months	9 months	12 months
ARS/USD	0.628	0.746	0.695	0.659
BOB/USD	2.795	3.501	4.245	4.517
BRL/USD	0.844	0.902	0.905	0.900
CLP/USD	0.808	0.908	0.919	0.919
COP/USD	0.775	0.895	0.935	0.938
PEN/USD	0.595	0.710	0.651	0.615
PYG/USD	0.862	0.970	1.013	1.048
PYG/BRL	0.705	0.842	0.850	0.832
PYG/ARS	0.730	0.830	0.808	0.777

Panel B: Root Mean Square Error (RMSE)

	3 months	6 months	9 months	12 months
ARS/USD	0.003	0.011	0.018	0.026
BOB/USD	0.000	0.000	0.000	0.001
BRL/USD	0.004	0.012	0.021	0.029
CLP/USD	0.001	0.003	0.006	0.008
COP/USD	0.003	0.008	0.013	0.020
PEN/USD	0.003	0.010	0.016	0.023
PYG/USD	0.002	0.006	0.009	0.012
PYG/BRL	0.004	0.015	0.027	0.036
PYG/ARS	0.005	0.015	0.024	0.032

Panel C: DoC

	3 months	6 months	9 months	12 months
ARS/USD	0.796	0.674	0.707	0.843
BOB/USD	0.594	0.443	0.482	0.426
BRL/USD	0.469	0.484	0.424	0.461
CLP/USD	0.531	0.453	0.511	0.506
COP/USD	0.490	0.516	0.533	0.551
PEN/USD	0.786	0.695	0.717	0.865
PYG/USD	0.531	0.453	0.587	0.427
PYG/BRL	0.582	0.526	0.598	0.551
PYG/ARS	0.612	0.526	0.511	0.573

Table 5 summarizes the out-of-sample (OOS) ratio of the BVAR RMSE over the random walk RMSE, its RMSE, and its DoC. The exchange rates assessed are ARS/USD, BOB/USD, BLR/USD, CLP/USD, COP/USD, PEN/USD, PYG/USD, PYG/BRL, and PYG/ARS. Panel A reports the RMSE ratios, panel B reports the RMSEs, and panel C reports the DoC ratios. The table summarizes the result for four horizons: $h = 3, 6, 9$, and 12 months. Under the RMSE criterion, a number lower than 1 means that the model in the row predicts better than the random walk benchmark. Under the DoC criterion, a ratio greater than 0.5 indicates that the model is outperforming the random walk.

6.3 Comparing Models using DoC

Tables 1, 2, 3, 4, and 5 also show the ratios of DoC for the exchange rates we are examining. Under this criterion, we evaluate if the model can "guess" whether the actual exchange rate increases or decreases. As previously mentioned, a random walk will correctly predict the direction of change half the time (an expected value of 0.5), so we will evaluate our forecasts against this benchmark.

Panel C in Table 1 displays the DoC ratios for the PPP model. Here we see that in the 3-month horizon, five exchange rates' direction of change is better predicted by the model: ARS/USD, BOB/USD, BRL/USD, PEN/USD, and PYG/BRL. In the 6-month horizon, the model outperforms the random walk in eight of the nine exchange rates (PYG/USD being the exception). In the 9-month horizon, the exceptions are BRL/USD and COP/USD, meaning the model does better in seven out of nine cases. In the 12-month horizon, PPP beats the random walk for all nine exchange rates.

Table 2, panel C, shows the DoC ratios for the UIP model. Under DoC, this model outperforms the random walk in the 3-month horizon in six out of nine cases, with the exception of CLP/USD, COP/USD, and PYG/USD. For the following horizon, UIP beats the random walk in seven out of nine instances, the exceptions being BOB/USD and PYG/USD. Nine months ahead, UIP fails in four cases: BOB/USD, BRL/USD, PYG/USD, and PYG/ARS. Finally, in the last horizon, UIP beats the random walk in all cases except BOB/USD.

In panel C of Table 3, we find the DoC ratios for the SP model. The direction of change is better predicted for six out of the nine exchange rates in the 3-month horizon – the exceptions being CLP/USD, PYG/USD, and PYG/ARS. It is predicted better for seven exchange rates 6 months ahead, save for BOB/USD and PYG/USD. In the 9-month horizon, SP underperforms for the BOB/USD, PYG/BRL, and PYG/ARS exchange rates. In the following forecasting period, SP fares even worse, beating the random walk in five out of nine cases: ARS/USD, PEN/USD, PYG/USD, PYG/BRL, and PYG/ARS.

The DoC ratios for BMA are displayed on panel C in Table 4. Here we see that in the first forecasting period, BMA beats the random walk for every exchange rate we are considering. Almost the same result is observed in the 6-month horizon, where the only exception is the PYG/USD exchange rate. In the 9-month horizon, BMA fails in two cases, namely, BRL/USD and PYG/USD. In the last forecasting horizon, BMA again outperforms the random walk for all exchange rates except PYG/USD.

In panel C in Table 5, we find the DoC ratios for the BVAR model. In this case, we find that this model outperforms the random walk for all exchange rates except two in the 3-month horizon (BRL/USD and COP/USD). In the 6-month horizon, BVAR fails at better predicting the direction of change in the cases of BOB/USD, BRL/USD, CLP/USD, and PYG/USD.

In the following period, the exceptions are the BOB/USD and BRL/USD exchange rates. Finally, in the 12-month horizon, BVAR does better than the random walk in six of out nine cases, the exceptions being BOB/USD, BRL/USD, and PYG/USD.

6.4 Comparing Models Using the DM Statistic

To see if the forecasts produced by some of the models are statistically significantly different and better than those produced by the random walk, these forecasts are compared using the Diebold-Mariano (DM) statistic. In Tables 6, 7, 8, 9, and 10, we present the DM statistics and the p-values for every forecasting horizon for PPP, UIP, SP, BMA, and BVAR, respectively. Recall that the null here is that of no difference between the forecasts.

From Table 6, we can see that PPP produces statistically significant improvements on the random walk forecasts only for the ARS/USD and PYG/ARS exchange rates. The former are statistically significant at the 10 percent level for the 3 to 9 months ahead periods, and at the 5 percent level for the 12 months ahead period. The latter are statistically significant at the 5 percent level in the first three forecasting horizons, and at the 1 percent level in the 12-month horizon. Any other improvements are not statistically significant.

In Table 7, we find that UIP produces statistically significantly better forecasts only in some instances. For the ARS/USD exchange rate, the 3-month and 12-month improvements are statistically significant at the 5 and 1 percent levels, respectively. Following Lothian and Wu (2011) in seeing a two-year horizon as the "start" of the long run, we include a 24-month forecasting period to see if UIP forecasts become better at this point. They do, but, again, the improvements are statistically significant only for ARS/USD at the 5 percent level, PYG/BRL at the 10 percent level, and PYG/ARS at the 10 percent level, as well (but very close to the 5 percent threshold). In the same horizon, the improved forecasts for BRL/USD and PYG/USD are also close to the 10 percent level. Any other improvements are not statistically significant.

Table 8 presents the results for the SP model. We find here that this model only seems to work well for the PYG/ARS exchange rate, where forecasts improve at a statistically significant level beginning in the 6-month period (at 5 percent) and continuing in the 9- and 12-month periods – at the 1 percent level in both cases. Only the 12-month horizon forecast for the ARS/USD exchange rate is close to statistical significance. Otherwise, any other improvements are not statistically significant.

Table 6 Diebold-Mariano (DM) tests for the PPP model

	ARS/USD	BOB/USD	BRL/USD	CLP/USD	COP/USD	PEN/USD	PYG/USD	PYG/BRL	PYG/ARS
3 months									
DM statistic	−1.378	6.166	0.138	0.824	0.279	−0.715	0.135	1.668	−1.832
p-value	0.0841	1.0000	0.5547	0.7951	0.6100	0.2374	0.5536	0.9524	0.0335
6 months									
DM statistic	−1.487	4.623	−0.181	0.915	0.622	−0.136	0.403	1.819	−1.624
p-value	0.0686	1.0000	0.4282	0.8200	0.7331	0.4460	0.6566	0.9655	0.0522
9 months									
DM statistic	−1.522	4.434	−0.521	0.625	0.909	0.125	0.458	1.520	−1.939
p-value	0.0640	1.0000	0.3013	0.7339	0.8183	0.5498	0.6765	0.9357	0.0263
12 months									
DM statistic	−1.649	4.879	−0.750	0.279	0.846	0.322	0.461	1.002	−2.868
p-value	0.0495	1.0000	0.2266	0.6099	0.8013	0.6262	0.6776	0.8419	0.0021

Table 6 summarizes the out-of-sample (OOS) Diebold-Mariano (DM) tests for the PPP model and for all the currencies under examination. The forecasting periods are 3, 6, 9, and 12 months ahead. The table reports the DM statistic and the corresponding p-value. Recall that the null hypothesis for the DM test is that there is no difference between the forecasts being compared.

Table 7 Diebold-Mariano (DM) tests for the UIP model

	ARS/USD	BOB/USD	BRL/USD	CLP/USD	COP/USD	PEN/USD	PYG/USD	PYG/BRL	PYG/ARS
3 months									
DM statistic	-1.759	3.191	1.177	1.508	0.403	2.612	-0.279	0.757	-0.175
p-value	0.0393	0.9993	0.8805	0.9343	0.6564	0.9955	0.3902	0.7753	0.4306
6 months									
DM statistic	-0.585	2.504	0.605	1.574	0.686	2.000	-0.465	1.321	1.270
p-value	0.2794	0.9939	0.7275	0.9422	0.7537	0.9772	0.3210	0.9068	0.8979
9 months									
DM statistic	-0.948	2.444	0.159	1.506	0.896	1.671	-0.589	1.269	1.487
p-value	0.1716	0.9927	0.5632	0.9339	0.8148	0.9526	0.2780	0.8979	0.9315
12 months									
DM statistic	-2.337	2.588	-0.304	1.215	0.824	1.475	-0.677	0.615	1.067
p-value	0.0097	0.9952	0.3807	0.8879	0.7951	0.9298	0.2492	0.7308	0.8571
24 months									
DM statistic	-2.062	3.437	-0.935	0.465	0.524	-0.004	-0.881	-1.386	-1.563
p-value	0.020	0.9997	0.1748	0.6791	0.6998	0.4984	0.1891	0.0829	0.0590

Table 7 summarizes the out-of-sample (OOS) Diebold-Mariano (DM) tests for the UIP model and for all the currencies under examination. The forecasting periods are 3, 6, 9, 12, and 24 months ahead. The table reports the DM statistic and the corresponding p-value. Recall that the null hypothesis for the DM test is that there is no difference between the forecasts being compared.

Table 8 Diebold-Mariano (DM) tests for the SP model

	ARS/USD	BOB/USD	BRL/USD	CLP/USD	COP/USD	PEN/USD	PYG/USD	PYG/BRL	PYG/ARS
3 months									
DM statistic	−0.364	6.438	1.040	1.747	1.087	−0.010	0.572	2.111	−0.036
p-value	0.3580	10.000	0.8509	0.9597	0.8615	0.4959	0.7163	0.9826	0.4856
6 months									
DM statistic	−0.005	4.759	0.756	1.670	1.290	1.186	0.596	2.059	−2.122
p-value	0.4980	1.0000	0.7751	0.9526	0.9014	0.8821	0.7243	0.9803	0.0169
9 months									
DM statistic	−0.195	4.448	0.648	1.513	1.590	1.718	0.595	1.921	−3.301
p-value	0.4228	1.0000	0.7415	0.9349	0.9441	0.9571	0.7240	0.9726	0.0005
12 months									
DM Statistic	−0.998	4.926	0.504	1.202	1.357	1.871	0.557	1.641	−4.068
p-value	0.1591	1.0000	0.6928	0.8854	0.9125	0.9693	0.7112	0.9496	0.0000

Table 8 summarizes the out-of-sample (OOS) Diebold-Mariano (DM) tests for the SP model and for all the currencies under examination. The forecasting periods are 3, 6, 9, and 12 months ahead. The table reports the DM statistic and the corresponding p-value. Recall that the null hypothesis for the DM test is that there is no difference between the forecasts being compared.

Table 9 Diebold-Mariano (DM) tests for the BMA model

	ARS/USD	BOB/USD	BRL/USD	CLP/USD	COP/USD	PEN/USD	PYG/USD	PYG/BRL	PYG/ARS
3 months									
DM Statistic	-0.387	2.837	-0.383	0.106	-1.736	-0.733	-0.655	-1.779	0.953
p-value	0.3493	0.9977	0.3508	0.5423	0.0413	0.2317	0.2563	0.0376	0.8296
6 months									
DM Statistic	-0.913	2.294	-0.441	0.356	-1.045	-1.478	0.263	-1.688	0.065
p-value	0.1807	0.9891	0.3295	0.6391	0.1480	0.0697	0.6036	0.0457	0.5261
9 months									
DM Statistic	-1.663	1.990	0.382	0.293	-0.862	-1.496	0.985	-2.146	-0.178
p-value	0.0482	0.9767	0.6488	0.6151	0.1943	0.0673	0.8378	0.0160	0.4295
12 months									
DM Statistic	-1.976	2.062	0.354	0.506	-1.205	-1.427	1.175	-3.248	-0.504
p-value	0.0241	0.9804	0.6383	0.6935	0.1142	0.0767	0.8800	0.0006	0.3072

Table 9 summarizes the out-of-sample (OOS) Diebold-Mariano (DM) tests for the BMA model and for all the currencies under examination. The forecasting periods are 3, 6, 9, and 12 months ahead. The table reports the DM statistic and the corresponding p-value. Recall that the null hypothesis for the DM test is that there is no difference between the forecasts being compared.

Table 10 Diebold-Mariano (DM) tests for the BVAR model

	ARS/USD	BOB/USD	BRL/USD	CLP/USD	COP/USD	PEN/USD	PYG/USD	PYG/BRL	PYG/ARS
3 months									
DM Statistic	−1.248	3.238	−0.701	−2.167	−2.336	−1.233	−2.265	−2.357	−2.633
p-value	0.1060	0.9994	0.2416	0.0151	0.0097	0.1088	0.0118	0.0092	0.0042
6 months									
DM Statistic	−1.782	2.820	−0.429	−1.328	−1.365	−1.501	−0.300	−2.635	−2.609
p-value	0.0374	0.9976	0.3339	0.0920	0.0862	0.0667	0.3821	0.0042	0.0045
9 months									
DM Statistic	−1.725	2.993	−0.306	−0.979	−1.008	−1.580	0.143	−4.183	−3.847
p-value	0.0423	0.9986	0.3799	0.1637	0.1568	0.0570	0.5569	0.0000	0.0001
12 months									
DM Statistic	−1.718	3.874	−0.326	−0.898	−1.185	−1.656	0.304	−5.331	−4.774
p-value	0.0429	0.9999	0.3724	0.1846	0.1179	0.0489	0.6195	0.0000	0.0000

Table 10 summarizes the out-of-sample (OOS) Diebold-Mariano (DM) tests for the BMA model and for all the currencies under examination. The forecasting periods are 3, 6, 9, and 12 months ahead. The table reports the DM statistic and the corresponding p-value. Recall that the null hypothesis for the DM test is that there is no difference between the forecasts being compared.

The results contained in Table 9 indicate that only a few improvements are statistically significant: in the 3-month horizon, we find COP/USD and PYG/BRL, both at the 5 percent level; in the 6-month horizon, we find PEN/USD and PYG/BRL at the 10 and 5 percent levels, respectively; in the 9-month horizon, we find ARS/USD and PYG/URL at the 5 and 1 percent levels, respectively; and in the 12-month horizon, we find ARS/USD and PEN/USD at the 1 and 5 percent levels, respectively (COP/USD is very close to the 10 percent level).

Finally, in Table 10 we find the results for the BVAR model, where statistically significant improvements are scattered in every forecasting horizon – the 12-month horizon having the most with four. In the 3-month horizon, the COP/USD and PYG/BRL forecasts are statistically significant improvements at the 5 percent level; in the 6-month horizon, the PEN/USD and PYG/BRL forecasts are statistically significant at the 10 and 5 percent levels, respectively; in the 9-month horizon, the ARS/USD, PEN/USD, and PYG/BRL forecasts are statistically significant improvements at the 5, 10, and 5 percent levels, respectively; in the 12-month horizon, the ARS/USD, PEN/USD, and PYG/BRL are statistically significant improvements at the 5, 10, and 1 percent levels (COP/USD is very close to the 10 percent threshold with a p-value of 0.11).

6.5 Discussion

The results shown are encouraging but mixed. Model performance diverges depending on the criterion under which they are evaluated. There is some evidence in favor of certain models, especially under RMSE and DoC and in particular for the BVAR model, but no model produces improved forecasts with consistent statistical significance – hence, the "mixed" character of the results.

As previously referred to in Section 2, some studies indicate that PPP has better long-run performance. Under the RMSE and DoC criteria, that seems to be the case, indeed. For the 12-month horizon, PPP presents RMSE ratios smaller than 1 in five out of nine cases and predicts the direction of change of the exchange rates better than the random walk in every case. However, as mentioned in the previous section, only some of these improvements are statistically significant.

In a similar case to PPP, the UIP model also appears to perform better in the longer forecasting horizons. The RMSE ratios are smaller than 1 in four cases and UIP outperforms the random walk in predicting the direction of change in all but one case. The statistical significance of this better performance is scattered, though. Even when we include a 24-month horizon, we find that only three of the nine forecasts are statistically significantly better. This last result, in particular, seems to argue against the use of UIP for the long run (although, in a previous version of this same experiment, with a different partition for IS and OOS but with fewer exchange rates, results indicated that UIP performed much better in longer horizons. Those results are not included here, however).

Under the RMSE criterion, the SP model appears to be the worst-performing model either in the short or the long run, according to the results presented in Section 5. It only produces ratios smaller than 1 in two out of nine cases in all forecasting horizons. Under the DoC criterion, it fares better, especially in the shorter forecasting horizons, outperforming the random walk in six and seven out of nine cases, for the 3-month and 6-month horizons, respectively. This flies in the face of previous studies that argued that monetary fundamentals models are better suited for the longer run. As might be expected, statistical significance is almost non-existent and found only for the PYG/ARS exchange rate.

Although we might expect the BMA model to function better in the short run, it beats the random walk with remarkable consistency in every forecasting horizon. Under the RMSE criterion, it produces a ratio smaller than 1 in six out of nine cases in every period. Under the DoC criterion, it under-performs the random walk only once in the last three forecasting horizons and not once in the 3-month horizon. As described in Section 5, there are also more instances of statistical significance in the improvements of the forecasts: three in 3-month horizon, four in the 6-, 9-, and 12-month horizons.

The BVAR model is by quite a margin the best-performing model. It handily beats the random walk in every horizon for almost every exchange rate under the RMSE criterion – only the BOB/USD exchange rate's ratio is greater than 1 in every horizon. Under the DoC criterion, it outperforms the random walk in eight out of nine cases in the 3-month horizon, six out of eight cases in the 6-month horizon, seven out of nine in the 9-month horizon, and six out of nine cases in the 12-month horizon. It also presents the most statistically significant improvements in every horizon: four, six, four, and four in the 3-, 6-, 9-, and 12-month horizons, respectively.

We should also point out that PPP works particularly well for the ARS/USD exchange rate. One explanation may be that Argentina had a contentious history with inflation during the period under study, and its monetary and fiscal policies were rather volatile, so much so that publications such as *The Economist* refused to publish governmental data on inflation because it was considered highly inaccurate.[6] Eventually, as mentioned earlier, even the government stopped publishing its own CPI for a year. Therefore, investors might have been more keenly aware of price fluctuations in the Argentinian peso.

Another exchange rate with a peculiar behavior is that of BOB/USD. All five models produce terrible results under the RMSE criterion, but they all beat the

---

[6] See for instance *The Economist*. "Don't lie to me, Argentina" at www.economist.com/node/

random walk at least in one (and in two cases, every) forecasting horizon. This could be explained by the fact that since 2012, Bolivia has a de facto fixed exchange rate (see Kehoe et al. (2019)). As mentioned by Rossi (2013), it is possible for a model to consistently predict the correct direction of change while over-predicting the actual exchange rate. This seemingly contradictory result need not be so.

The evidence presented here seems to be heavily in favor of the two Bayesian models, especially BVAR. There is some evidence in favor of PPP, in particular in the 12-month horizon, but, in general, this experiment does not lend great support to fundamentals models.

6.6 Further Research

The present study could be expanded in different directions. First, the same models could be used to forecast the behavior of the all currencies here considered with respect to other relevant currencies, where available. Other models could also be considered for the currency exchange rates included in this work.

A note on the data opens another interesting, if improbable, avenue of research. Unlike certain works such as Koenig et al. (2003) and Croushore and Stark (2003), we do not use real-time data. These authors argue that some variables used on the right hand-side of an equation could become irrelevant if we were to use data of real-time vintage. Certainly, such an experiment could show how robust our findings here are, but something of that nature would be subject to data that is not currently available (to the best of these authors' knowledge). In similar terms, the priors used in the Bayesian models could be altered to see if there are changes in the results – for better or worse. Likewise, the size of the rolling window could be changed so as to compare results.

Another avenue of research could be the inclusion of other forecasting models and compare their performances to the benchmark model. Some possibilities include GARCH models (see, for instance, Pilbeam and Langeland (2015)) or copula models (see Cerrato et al. (2015)).

A more laborious possibility could involve the calculation of Divisia monetary aggregates for the countries that do not yet have them and then include them in the pertinent models. Barnett et al. (2005) have already used these aggregates in several structural models to forecast the exchange rate between the US dollar and the British pound. A similar experiment would be to include Divisia monetary aggregates in the Bayesian models to verify if they have a greater weight in forecasting exchange rates or if they can help in their improvement.

The availability of high-frequency data could also tell us more about the relationship between exchange rates and commodity prices, especially those traded in great volumes by South American countries.

7 Conclusion

The academic discussion on exchange rate forecasting has existed for more than a century. In all this time, the arguments for and against the possibility of actually being able to produce significant forecasts have gone back and forth, and the strength of either argument has ebbed and flowed, depending on the context. The conventional wisdom in the profession seems to be anchored in the idea that the Meese and Rogoff puzzle holds and that a consistent method of forecasting does not exist. In that sense, the present Element "goes against the grain" as it were, in arguing that we can contribute to finding the elusive forecasting methodology that will fit different contexts for emerging markets, in particular, those of South America.

Even if improvements are only contextual or partial, these methods can still be relevant for policy, and it is certainly preferable to doing nothing. For all the South American economies under study, exchange rates are a very important matter. Their main exports are traded in highly dollarized markets.

The results we have obtained here seem to validate some of the results in previous studies, such as those mentioned in Rossi (2013): the evidence in favor of the use of the UIP model is poor, especially in the short run; traditional predictors such as those used in the SP model do not perform well; there is limited evidence in favor of the PPP model for longer forecasting horizons. In this sense, results in this Element also contradict some of the results mentioned in the same paper, as we find that Bayesian models, especially BVAR, perform very well. The latter, in particular, is the only one that outperforms the random walk under every criterion.

From the evidence here presented, then, the takeaways seem to be twofold: on the one hand, more traditional fundamentals models do not perform as well when compared with a random walk; on the other hand, Bayesian models appear to do much better against the same benchmark, which is the encouraging part of the results. Perhaps the former situation does arise from what Engel et al. (2007) propose when they express their reservations with respect to the use of the random walk as a benchmark: we may be asking too much from models that produce forecasts with a random walk–like behavior. Whatever the case, forecasting exchange rates does not look like a lost cause and further research could help shed light on the matter.

8 Graphs

The following graphs display the forecasts of each of the five models against the actual (or realized) exchange rate for all nine bilateral exchange rates considered in this Element.

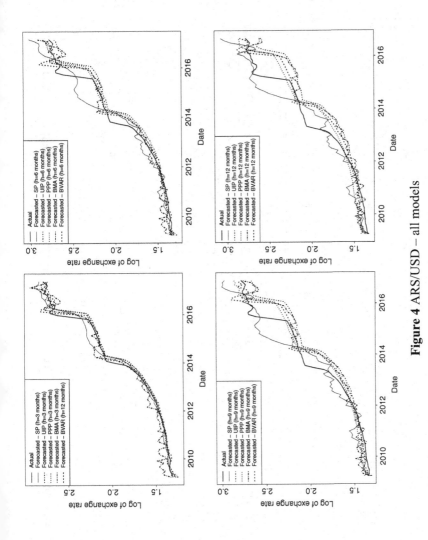

Figure 4 ARS/USD – all models

Figure 4 shows all five models' forecasts plotted against the realized (or actual) ARS/USD exchange rates.

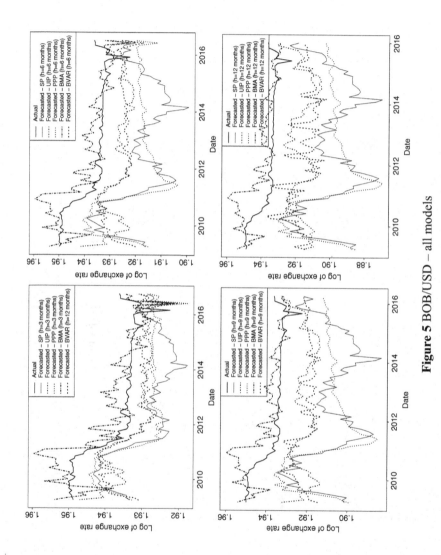

Figure 5 BOB/USD – all models

Figure 5 shows all five models' forecasts plotted against the realized (or actual) BOB/USD exchange rates.

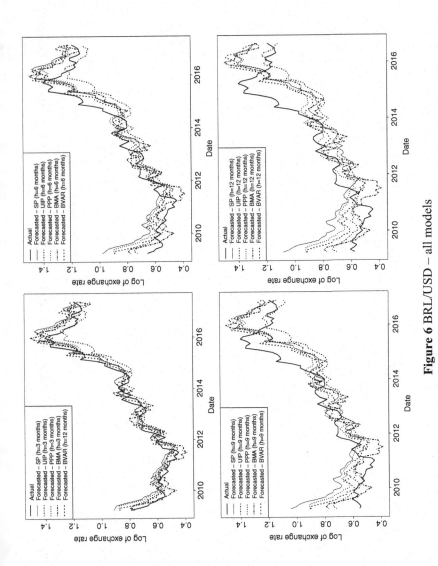

Figure 6 BRL/USD – all models

Figure 6 shows all five models' forecasts plotted against the realized (or actual) BRL/USD exchange rates.

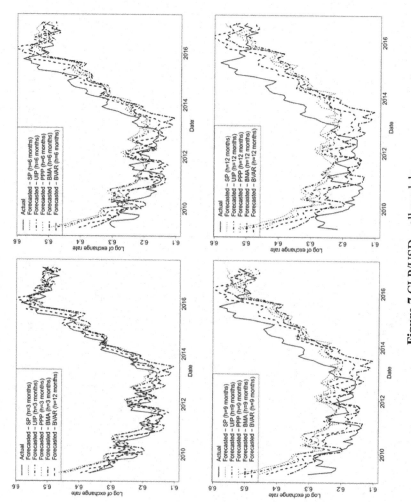

Figure 7 CLP/USD – all models

Figure 7 shows all five models' forecasts plotted against the realized (or actual) CLP/USD exchange rates.

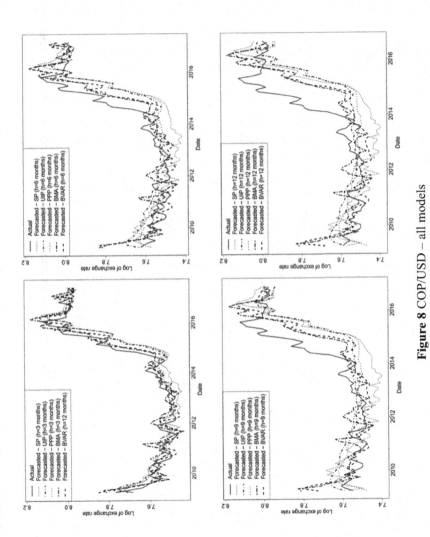

Figure 8 COP/USD – all models

Figure 8 shows all five models' forecasts plotted against the realized (or actual) COP/USD exchange rates.

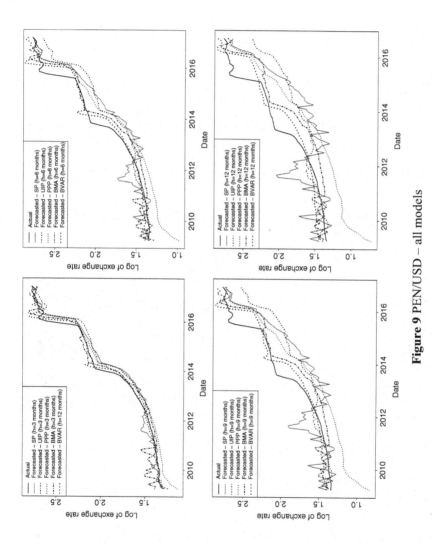

Figure 9 PEN/USD – all models

Figure 9 shows all five models' forecasts plotted against the realized (or actual) PEN/USD exchange.

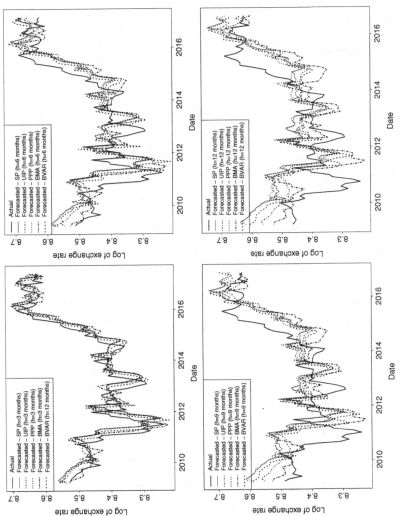

Figure 10 PYG/USD – all models

Figure 10 shows all five models' forecasts plotted against the realized (or actual) PYG/USD exchange rates.

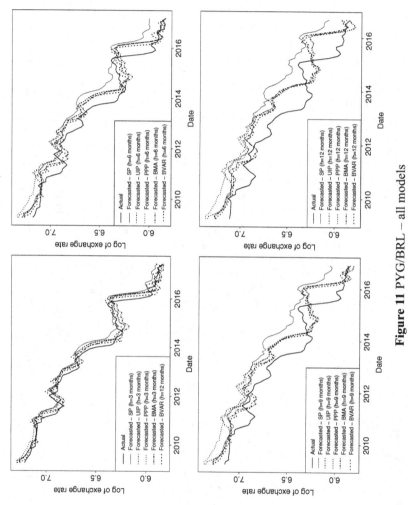

Figure 11 PYG/BRL – all models

Figure 11 shows all five models' forecasts plotted against the realized (or actual) PYG/BRL exchange rates.

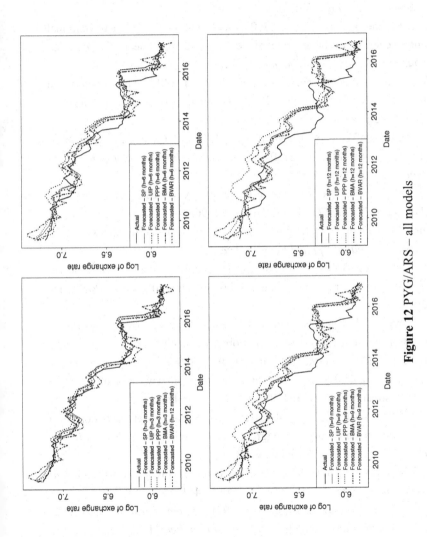

Figure 12 PYG/ARS – all models

Figure 12 shows all five models' forecasts plotted against the realized (or actual) PYG/ARS exchange rates.

References

Abhyankar, A., Sarno, L., and Valente, G. (2005). Exchange rates and fundamentals: Evidence on the economic value of predictability. *Journal of International Economics*, 66(2): 325–48.

Alquist, R. and Chinn, M. D. (2008). Conventional and unconventional approaches to exchange rate modelling and assessment. *International Journal of Finance & Economics*, 13(1): 2–13.

Ayres, J., Garcia, M., Guill´en, D. A., and Kehoe, P. J. (2019). The monetary and fiscal history of Brazil, 1960–2016. Technical report, National Bureau of Economic Research.

Bacchetta, P., Van Wincoop, E., and Beutler, T. (2009). Can parameter instability explain the Meese-Rogoff puzzle? *NBER International Seminar on Macroeconomics*, 6: 125–73. JSTOR.

Balassa, B. (1964). The purchasing-power parity doctrine: A reappraisal. *Journal of Political Economy*, 72(6): 584–96.

Banbura, M., Giannone, D., and Reichlin, L. (2007). Bayesian vars with large panels. *Journal of Applied Econometrics*, 25.

Banco Central de Bolivia. La Historia del Banco Central de Bolivia. (n. d.). Retrieved from www.bcb.gob.bo/?q=Las%20Reformas%20del%2070

Banco Central de la República Argentina. (BCRA). (n.d.). Historia del Banco Central. Retrieved from www.bcra.gob.ar/Institucional/Historia.asp

Banco Central de la Reserva del Peru. (2000). Memoria Anual. Banco Central de la Reserva del Perú. Lima, Perú. Retrieved from www.repositorio.cepal .org/bitstream/handle/11362/40402/1/RV E119Chacaltana.pdf

Barnett, W. A., Kwag, C. H., et al. (2005). Exchange rate determination from monetary fundamentals: An aggregation theoretic approach. *Frontiers in Finance and Economics*, 3(1): 29–48.

Bates, J. M. and Granger, C. W. (1969). The combination of forecasts. *Journal of the Operational Research Society*, 20(4): 451–68.

Baumann, R. and Fialho Mussi, C. H. (1999). *Algunas características de la economía brasileña desde la adopción del Plan Real*. Temas de coyuntura. N° 5 . ECLAC.

Berkowitz, J. and Giorgianni, L. (2001). Long-horizon exchange rate predictability? *Review of Economics and Statistics*, 83(1): 81–91.

Bernanke, B. S. and Boivin, J. (2003). Monetary policy in a data-rich environment. *Journal of Monetary Economics*, 50(3): 525–46.

Buera, F. J. and Nicolini, J. P. (2019). The monetary and fiscal history of Argentina: 1960–2017. University of Chicago, Becker Friedman Institute for Economics Working Paper.

Cagan, P. (1956). The monetary dynamics of hyperinflation. In *Studies in the Quantity Theory of Money*. Chicago: University of Chicago Press, 25–117.

Canto, J. P. (1942). El sistema monetario de chile. *Revista de Economía y Estadística*, 4(4): 487–517.

Caputo, R. and Saravia, D. (2018). The monetary and fiscal history of Chile: 1960–2016. University of Chicago, Becker Friedman Institute for Economics Working Paper, 62.

Carriero, A., Kapetanios, G., and Marcellino, M. (2009). Forecasting exchange rates with a large Bayesian VAR. *International Journal of Forecasting*, 25 (2): 400–417.

Cassel, G. (1918a). Abnormal deviations in international exchanges. *The Economic Journal*, 28(112): 413–15.

Central Bank of Bolivia. (2018). *Reseña Histórica de Monedas y Billetes de Bolivia." Nuestra Economía al alcance de todos*. Vol. 13. Retrieved from www.bcb.gob.bo/webdocs/seccioneducativa/Boletin%20BCB%20N13.pdf

Cerra, V. and Saxena, S. C. (2010). The monetary model strikes back: Evidence from the world. *Journal of International Economics*, 81(2): 184–96.

Cerrato, M., Crosby, J., Kim, M., and Zhao, Y. (2015). Modeling dependence structure and forecasting market risk with dynamic asymmetric copula. Available at SSRN 2460168.

Chamon, M. M., Hofman, M. D. J., Magud, M. N. E., and Werner, A. M. (2019). *Foreign exchange intervention in inflation targeters in Latin America*. Washington, DC: International Monetary Fund.

Charotti, C. J., Fernández-Valdovinos, C., and Gonzalez Soley, F. (2019). The monetary and fiscal history of Paraguay, 1960–2017. University of Chicago, Becker Friedman Institute for Economics Working Paper.

Cheung, Y.-W., Chinn, M. D., and Pascual, A. G. (2005). Empirical exchange rate models of the nineties: Are any fit to survive? *Journal of International Money and Finance*, 24(7): 1150–75.

Cheung, Y.-W., Chinn, M. D., Pascual, A. G., and Zhang, Y. (2019). Exchange rate prediction redux: New models, new data, new currencies. *Journal of International Money and Finance*, 95: 332–62.

Chinn, M. D. (1991). Some linear and nonlinear thoughts on exchange rates. *Journal of International Money and Finance*, 10(2): 214–30.

Chinn, M. D. and Meese, R. A. (1995). Banking on currency forecasts: How predictable is change in money? *Journal of International Economics*, 38 (1–2): 161–78.

Clark, T. E. and West, K. D. (2006). Using out-of-sample mean squared prediction errors to test the martingale difference hypothesis. *Journal of Econometrics*, 135(1–2): 155–86.

Corbo, V. and Hernañdez, L. (2005). Ochenta años de historia del Banco Central de Chile. *Documentos de Trabajo (Banco Central de Chile)*, 345: 1.

Croushore, D. and Stark, T. (2003). A real-time data set for macroeconomists: Does the data vintage matter? *Review of Economics and Statistics*, 85(3): 605–17.

Dargent, E. (2018). La Moneda en el Peru: 450 años de historia. Retrieved from http://vbeta.urp.edu.pe/pdf/id/17007/n/la-moneda-en-el-peru-2205-23-feb-2019.pdf

Diebold, F. X. and Mariano, R. S. (1995). Comparing predictive accuracy. *Journal of Business & Economic Statistics*, 13(3): 253–63.

Dimand, R. W. and Gomez Betancourt, R. (2012). Retrospectives: Irving Fisher's appreciation and interest (1896) and the Fisher relation. *Journal of Economic Perspectives*, 26(4): 185–96.

Dornbusch, R. (1976). Expectations and exchange rate dynamics. *Journal of Political Economy*, 84(6): 1161–76.

Edge, R. M., Kiley, M. T., and Laforte, J.-P. (2010). A comparison of forecast performance between Federal Reserve staff forecasts, simple reduced-form models, and a DSGE model. *Journal of Applied Econometrics*, 25(4): 720–54.

Engel, C. (1994). Can the Markov switching model forecast exchange rates? *Journal of International Economics*, 36(1–2): 151–65.

Engel, C., Mark, N. C., West, K. D., Rogoff, K., and Rossi, B. (2007). Exchange rate models are not as bad as you think [with comments and discussion]. *NBER Macroeconomics Annual*, 22: 381–473.

Engel, C. and West, K. D. (2005). Exchange rates and fundamentals. *Journal of Political Economy*, 113(3): 485–517.

Faust, J., Rogers, J. H., and Wright, J. H. (2003). Exchange rate forecasting: The errors we've really made. *Journal of International Economics*, 60(1): 35–59.

Fernández Valdovinos, C. and Monge Naranjo, A. (2003). Economic growth in Paraguay. *Economic and Social Study Series*. Inter-American Development Bank.

Ferraro, D., Rogoff, K., and Rossi, B. (2015). Can oil prices forecast exchange rates? An empirical analysis of the relationship between commodity prices and exchange rates. *Journal of International Money and Finance*, 54: 116–41.

French-Davis, R. (2003). Chile, entre el neoliberalismo y el crecimiento con equidad. *Nueva Sociedad*, 183: 70–90.

Fisher, I. (1896). *Appreciation and interest: A study of the influence of monetary appreciation and depreciation on the rate of interest with applications to the bimetallic controversy and the theory of interest*, vol. 11. New York: American Economic Association.

Fontaine, J. A. (1993). Transición económica y política en Chile:1970–1990. *Estudios Públicos*, 50: 229–79.

Frankel, J. A. (1979). On the mark: A theory of floating exchange rates based on real interest differentials. *The American Economic Review*, 69(4): 610–22.

(1982). The mystery of the multiplying marks: A modification of the monetary model. *The Review of Economics and Statistics*, 64(3): 515–19.

Frankel, J. A. and Rose, A. K. (1994). A survey of empirical research on nominal exchange rates. Technical report, National Bureau of Economic Research.

Frenkel, J. A. (1976). A monetary approach to the exchange rate: doctrinal aspects and empirical evidence. *The Scandinavian Journal of Economics*, 78: 200–24.

Froot, K. A. and Rogoff, K. (1995). Perspectives on PPP and long-run real exchange rates. *Handbook of International Economics*, 3: 1647–88.

Froot, K. A. and Thaler, R. H. (1990). Anomalies: Foreign exchange. *Journal of Economic Perspectives*, 4(3): 179–92.

Ghosh, T. and Bhadury, S. (2018). Money's causal role in exchange rate: Do Divisia monetary aggregates explain more? *International Review of Economics & Finance*, 57: 402–17.

Gourinchas, P.-O. and Rey, H. (2007). International financial adjustment. *Journal of Political Economy*, 115(4): 665–703.

Gozzi, E. and Tappatá, R. (2010). Primera iniciativa de reforma financiera profunda en América Latina la misión Kemmerer. *Fitproper:* www.fitproper.com/doc umentos/propios/Mision_Kemmerer.pdf. Accessed January 6, 2017.

Hoeting, J. A., Madigan, D., Raftery, A. E., and Volinsky, C. T. (1999). Bayesian model averaging: A tutorial. *Statistical Science*, 14(4): 382–401.

Hooper, P. and Morton, J. (1982). Fluctuations in the dollar: A model of nominal and real exchange rate determination. *Journal of International Money and Finance*, 1: 39–56.

Hsing, Y. and Sergi, B. S. (2009). The dollar/euro exchange rate and a comparison of major models. *Journal of Business Economics and Management*, 10(3): 199–205.

Humerez Quiroz, J. and Ayaviri, M. M. (2005). Sostenibilidad y gestión de la deuda pública externa. *Análisis Económico Volumen*, 20.

Insfrán Pelozo, J. A. (2003). El sector financiero paraguayo. Evaluando 10 años de transición (liberalización y crisis). *The Paraguayan Financial Sector. An assessment of.* Series Enfoques, Centro Paraguayo para la Promoción de la Libertad Económica y de la Justicia Social (CEPPRO). No. 26, April

International Monetary Fund. (2001). Silent revolution: The IMF 1979–1989, Chapter 9 – Containing the crisis, 1983–85. Retrieved from www.imf.org /external/pubs/ft/history/2001/index.htm

Jaramillo, J. C., Steiner, R., and Salazar, N. (1999). The political economy of exchange rate policy in Colombia. (No. 3064). Inter-American Development Bank, Research Department.

Kehoe, T. J., Machicado, C. G., and Peres-Caj´ıas, J. (2019). The monetary and fiscal history of bolivia, 1960–2017. Technical report, National Bureau of Economic Research.

Keynes, J. M. (1923). *A tract on monetary reform.* London: Macmillan.

Kilian, L. and Taylor, M. P. (2003). Why is it so difficult to beat the random walk forecast of exchange rates? *Journal of International Economics*, 60(1): 85–107.

Koenig, E. F., Dolmas, S., and Piger, J. (2003). The use and abuse of real-time data in economic forecasting. *Review of Economics and Statistics*, 85(3): 618–28.

Ladefroux, R. (1994). Brasil: Consecuencias de los planes de estabilización sobre los problemas alimentarios. Retrieved from https://horizon .documentation.ird.fr/exl-doc/pleins_textes/divers17-07/42029.pdf

Lam, L., Fung, L., and Yu, I.-W. (2008). Comparing forecast performance of exchange rate models. Available at SSRN 1330705.

Lara, R., Pankow, M., Insfrán, H., Caballero, L., and Cantero, J. (2013). El Guaraní 70 Años de Estabilidad Una Conquista Social. Retrieved from: www.portalguarani.com/267_felix_toranzos_miers/4864_misione s_2008__obras_de_felix_toranzos.html

Leamer, E. E. (1978). *Specification searches: Ad hoc inference with nonexperimental data.* New York: Wiley.

Lebdioui, A. (2019). Chile's export diversification since 1960: A free market miracle or mirage? *Development and Change*, 50(6): 1624–63.

Lewis, K. K. (1994). Puzzles in international financial markets. Technical report, National Bureau of Economic Research.

Litterman, R. B. (1986). Forecasting with Bayesian vector autoregressions – five years of experience. *Journal of Business & Economic Statistics*, 4(1): 25–38.

Lothian, J. R. and Wu, L. (2011). Uncovered interest-rate parity over the past two centuries. *Journal of International Money and Finance*, 30(3): 448–73.

Malkiel, B. G. and Fama, E. F. (1970). Efficient capital markets: A review of theory and empirical work. *The Journal of Finance*, 25(2): 383–417.

Mark, N. C. (1995). Exchange rates and fundamentals: Evidence on long-horizon predictability. *American Economic Review*, 85(1): 201–18.

Marongiu, F. (2007). High inflation and adjustment in Brazil during the return to democracy – 1985–1994. *Munich Personal RePEc Archive*. Retrieved from http://mpra.ub. unimuenchen. de/18956/

Martinelli, C. and Vega, M. (2019). Experimentos Radicales de Política, Inflación y Estabilización. Retrieved from www.bcrp.gob.pe/docs/ Publicaciones/Documentos-de-Trabajo/2018/documento-detrabajo-007– 2018-esp.pdf

Meese, R. A. and Rogoff, K. (1983). Empirical exchange rate models of the seventies: Do they fit out of sample? *Journal of International Economics*, 14(1–2): 3–24.

Molodtsova, T. and Papell, D. H. (2009). Out-of-sample exchange rate predictability with Taylor rule fundamentals. *Journal of International Economics*, 77(2): 167–80.

Mortimore, M. (1981). El estado y los bancos transnacionales: enseñanza de la crisis boliviana de endeudamiento público externo. *Revista de la CEPAL*.

Mussa, M. (1977). The exchange rate, the balance of payments and monetary and fiscal policy under a regime of controlled floating. In *Flexible Exchange Rates and Stabilization Policy*, pages 97–116. London: Palgrave Macmillan.

National Institute of Statistics and Informatics (INEI). (2016). Panorama de la Economía Peruana. 1950–2015. Instituto Nacional de Estadística e Informática. Lima, Peru. Retrieved from www.inei.gob.pe/media/ MenuRecursivo/publicacionesdigitales/Est/Lib1359/index.html

Pereira, L. C. B. and Nakano, Y. (1991). Hyperinflation and stabilization in Brazil: The first Collor plan. In *Economic Problems of the 1990s*, edited by P. Davidson and J. Kregel. London: Edward Elgar, 41–68.

Perez-Reyna, D. and Osorio-Rodríguez, D. (2016). The fiscal and monetary history of Colombia: 1963–2012. Technical report, mimeo.

Pilbeam, K. and Langeland, K. N. (2015). Forecasting exchange rate volatility: Garch models versus implied volatility forecasts. *International Economics and Economic Policy*, 12(1): 127–42.

Raftery, A. E., Madigan, D., and Hoeting, J. A. (1997). Bayesian model averaging for linear regression models. *Journal of the American Statistical Association*, 92(437): 179–91.

Rossi, B. (2013). Exchange rate predictability. *Journal of Economic Literature*, 51(4): 1063–119.

Rossi, B. and Inoue, A. (2012). Out-of-sample forecast tests robust to the choice of window size. *Journal of Business & Economic Statistics*, 30 (3): 432–53.

Sachs, J. (1987). The Bolivian hyperinflation and stabilization. *The American Economic Review*, 77(2): 279–83.

Sánchez, F., Armenta, A., and Fernández, A. (2005). *Historia monetaria de Colombia en el siglo XX: grandes tendencias y episodios relevantes*. Number 30. Centro de Desarrollo Económico at the Universidad de los Andes in Colombia (CEDE).

Sarantis, N. (2006). On the short-term predictability of exchange rates: A BVAR time-varying parameters approach. *Journal of Banking & Finance*, 30(8): 2257–79.

Schüssler, R., Beckmann, J., Koop, G., and Korobilis, D. (2018). Exchange rate predictability and dynamic Bayesian learning. Essex Finance Centre Working Papers 20781, University of Essex, Essex Business School.

Sheriff, B. and Ernesto, H. (1992). Política económica, crecimiento y bienestar: Bolivia (1950–1990). CEPAL, 1992. Retrieved from: https://repositorio .cepal.org/handle/11362/28237

Singh, A. (2005). Stabilization and reform in Latin America: Macroeconomic perspective on the experience since the early 1990s. Technical report, International Monetary Fund.

Stock, J. H. and Watson, M. W. (2002). Forecasting using principal components from a large number of predictors. *Journal of the American Statistical Association*, 97(460): 1167–79.

(2004). Combination forecasts of output growth in a seven-country data set. *Journal of Forecasting*, 23(6): 405–30.

Theil, H. (1971). *Applied economic forecasting*. Chicago: North-Holland Publishing Company.

Van Dijk, D. and Franses, P. H. (2003). Selecting a nonlinear time series model using weighted tests of equal forecast accuracy. *Oxford Bulletin of Economics and Statistics*, 65: 727–44.

West, K. D. (1996). Asymptotic inference about predictive ability. *Econometrica: Journal of the Econometric Society*, 64(5): 1067–84.

Wieland, V. and Wolters, M. (2013). Forecasting and policy making. In *Handbook of Economic Forecasting*, vol. 2, edited by G. Elliott and A. Timmerman, pp. 239–325. New York: Elsevier.

World Bank. (2017). Peru – Systematic country diagnostic (English). Washington, DC: World Bank Group. Retrieved from www.documents.worldbank.org /curated/en/919181490109288624/Peru–Systematic–Country–Diagnostic

Wright, J. H. (2008). Bayesian model averaging and exchange rate forecasts. *Journal of Econometrics*, 146(2): 329–41.

Cambridge Elements ≡

Economics of Emerging Markets

Bruno S. Sergi

Harvard University

Editor Bruno S. Sergi is an Instructor at Harvard University, an Associate of the Harvard University Davis Center for Russian and Eurasian Studies and Harvard Ukrainian Research Institute. He is the Academic Series Editor of the Cambridge *Elements in the Economics of Emerging Markets* (Cambridge University Press), a co-editor of the *Lab for Entrepreneurship and Development* book series, and associate editor of *The American Economist*. Concurrently, he teaches International Economics at the University of Messina, Scientific Director of the Lab for Entrepreneurship and Development (LEAD), and a co-founder and Scientific Director of the International Center for Emerging Markets Research at RUDN University in Moscow. He has published over 150 articles in professional journals and twenty-one books as author, co-author, editor, and co-editor.

About the Series

The aim of this Elements series is to deliver state-of-the-art, comprehensive coverage of the knowledge developed to date, including the dynamics and prospects of these economies, focusing on emerging markets' economics, finance, banking, technology advances, trade, demographic challenges, and their economic relations with the rest of the world, as well as the causal factors and limits of economic policy in these markets.

Cambridge Elements ☰

Economics of Emerging Markets

Elements in the Series

Towards a Theory of "Smart" Social Infrastructures at Base of the Pyramid: A Study of India
Sandeep Goyal and Bruno S. Sergi

Exchange Rates in South America's Emerging Markets
Luis Molinas Sosa and Caio Vigo Pereira

A full series listing is available at: www.cambridge.org/EEM

Printed in the United States
By Bookmasters